DIGITAL SIMPLIFIED

Digital business enables growth, speed, & innovation

Digital transformation creates scale

Raj B. Vattikuti

Ram Charan

DIGITAL SIMPLIFIED

Digital business enables growth, speed, & innovation

Digital transformation creates scale

Published by Leadership Lit
Irvington, New York 10533 USA
An imprint of Imagine and Wonder.
www.LeadershipLit.com

Scan this QR code with your phone camera
for more titles from Imagine and Wonder

Your guarantee of quality
As publishers, we strive to produce every book to the highest commercial standards.
The printing and binding have been planned to ensure a sturdy, attractive publication
that should give years of enjoyment. If your copy fails to meet our high standards,
please inform us and we will gladly replace it. admin@imagineandwonder.com

ISBN: 9781637610619
Library of Congress Control Number: 2022938799

First Edition

Printed in the USA

LEADERSHIPLIT

Notes on the Authors

"As a technologist, entrepreneur and philanthropist, Raj Vattikuti has the ideal background to outline the steps of creating a Digital Strategy. Ram Charan is one of the world's most influential consultants who brings deep business insight and understanding of digital business. Together Raj and Ram explain the benefits and pitfalls of various approaches and why standing still means failure. This book explains how a digital business thinks, operates with agility, develops deeper customer relationships, and appropriately uses technology. It also emphasizes that developing a Digital Strategy is an ongoing process to sustain a competitive advantage and provides a template to help business compete in a digital economy. This book offers a practical perspective from decades of partnering with various businesses across many sectors and outlines how to create value for your customers and business."

Jacques Nasser AC

"Creating Digital businesses is an enduring and self-correcting outcome. A stand-alone digital transformation is much more transitory. Raj, a serial technology entrepreneur, has had vision and clarity on this distinction well before others did. Ram, a world-renowned business consultant, has been focused on cutting through complex business environments to help companies grow. This discourse on distinguishing between Digital Business and Digital Transformation is the best I have seen on creating lasting value and outcomes within enterprises by looking at things through a digital business lens. It is about leveraging existing systems, data and applications through an accelerated, collaborative and bite-sized process to drive change."

Manoj Singh, Chief Operating officer (Retd), Deloitte Global

"In their book, "Digital Business", Raj and Ram simplify the approach to building a digital business and provide an excellent framework for business leaders to unlock growth and deliver tangible results. I confidently recommend their framework and the Altimetrik approach, anchored in the single source of truth, powered by a state-of-the-art platform, driven by uniquely competent and talented executives to deliver real outcomes. It is a great approach to building a digital business!"

George Zoghbi, CEO, The Arnott's Group

"Raj Vattikuti shares his expertise as a digital business innovator and Ram Charan brings his extensive experience in working with the world's top companies and CEOs. This book is an essential guide for how successful teams work collaboratively to solve business challenges and deliver world-class digital solutions quickly. Regardless of company size or industry, this is a valuable guide that provides all the ingredients needed to undertake digital transformation and win."

Joyce Phillips, Founder & CEO, EqualFuture Corp.

"Raj Vattikuti and Ram Charan have seen what so many others have missed—real digital transformation starts and ends with the business. The central lessons of their book are what every leader needs to hear: Give digital ownership to the business. Take an agile, iterative approach to investment. Design an innovation process based on experimentation. Push for speed and build digital products in weeks, not years. Shift the culture towards empowering employees, collaborate across silos, and focus on outcomes. This is how digital transformation delivers lasting growth. If you are leading a legacy business today, you cannot afford anything less!"

David L. Rogers, global bestselling author of "The Digital Transformation Playbook"

"Making the linkage between digital business and digital transformation is often missed. Both are needed for growth although they are different. Bringing them together with an understanding and proficiency makes this book an essential read. Businesses taking the lead to focus on key outcomes through a bite-sized approach in a collaborative culture accelerate substantive growth. Companies will become more agile and profitable if they can harness the power of digital business. This book is a fantastic guide and invaluable tool for business and technology leaders"

Twinkle Gupta, Chief Product Officer, Access Information Management

"This book is a game changer: no longer will the IT department be seen as disconnected from digital imperatives. Data ultimately should determine the direction of business strategy, capital allocation, and how to assess competitive threats and opportunities. Raj and Ram present the business case for driving digital solutions through innovative IT platforms which keep the plane afloat while installing a new digital engine."

Dennis Carey, Vice Chairman Korn Ferry, Founder The Prium and The CEO-Academy

"'Digital' Simplified: Digital Business – Drive Growth | Digital Transformation – Create Scale" is a great analysis of the state of digital business and the issues that lie ahead for organizations. The book does a great job of using different case studies, giving the reader practical examples and ideas for actions. Following the initial introduction of the concepts of digital business, the chapters around simplification and agility and the chapter on innovation and experimentation provide excellent insights and case studies that will help organizations struggling with these issues as they scale their digital platforms. Lastly the chapter around self-service digital platforms provides insight into the evolution from project-based digital environments to product-based digital organizations. This chapter covers some of the key challenges organizations face the next three or four years as they transition to a digital product focus. The case studies reveal some of the challenges and learnings of early adopters.

This book will provide great insight for both senior IT leaders and business leaders. You will enjoy and learn from it."

Peter Sondergaard, CEO, The Sondergaard Group, Chairman of the Board DI2X, DecideAct & 2021.ai

DEDICATION

This book is dedicated to the practitioners that drive digital business change. You are an inspiration.

ACKNOWLEDGEMENTS

THE EVER-CHANGING NATURE OF TECHNOLOGY AND PROLIFERATION of data have been the catalyst for the extraordinary growth in the demand for digital business. Companies are literally reinventing themselves at an ever-increasing rate and frequency. Companies that embrace this new paradigm will find success, while those who do not will fall further and further behind.

We want to thank the practitioners who contributed to this book. They understand companies are dealing with complex challenges and struggle to implement the needed change in their own digital journey. They are industry experts working with companies across the globe helping to simplify business and technologies that bring speed, scale, and outcomes. We created this digital playbook to provide guidance, an approach, and real-world examples to help others achieve success in their own digital business transformation.

Special thanks are extended to Lakshmi Narasimhan Duvoor, Jeffrey Fleischman, Arun Kumar, Ganesh Raj Mohan P, Shubhabrata Mohanty, Sirish Mellacheruvu, Jayaprakash Nair, Farid Roshan, Aurobindo Sahoo, Scott Sandschafer, Ramamurthy Shama Shastry, Ravi Shetty, Raj Sundaresan, Ramji P Vasudevan, Vipul Valamjee, Abhinav Vattikuti, and Henk Vlietstra.

FOREWORD

I HAVE KNOWN RAJ VATTIKUTI AND RAM CHARAN FOR ALMOST
three decades. In some ways, we are about as different as you can imagine, but we also have many things in common. We are immigrants to
the U.S. with strong work ethics and a belief that successful communities
and a strong business environment go together. Also, we are focused
on how to improve the robustness and growth of business. When they
approached me for the concept of the book and the many benefits of
becoming a digital business, it made perfect sense. Raj and Ram had
a goal to share their collective knowledge and experience to produce
a digital business playbook and they achieved what they set out to do.

I met Raj when I was with the Ford Motor Company (I later became
CEO). At that stage he was already a successful founder, entrepreneur,
and thought leader. There is a special quality about Raj, and we have been
close friends and colleagues ever since. About the same time, I met Ram
who had earned a reputation as a trusted advisor to some of the world's
top executives. I have gotten to know Ram over the years and not only
has he become a trusted advisor, I'm also proud to call him my friend.

Raj has been successful in many fields and is a 21st Century mix of
technologist, entrepreneur, and philanthropist. As a young man, he
immigrated to the U.S. to further his studies at Wayne State University,

and early in his career, was with Chrysler in Detroit. Raj has not looked back since. As an entrepreneur he takes calculated risks and backs his own judgment. Throughout his career he has demonstrated thought leadership at the intersection of business - particularly as it relates to the appropriate use of technology, but also with the community at large.

Like many intelligent people, Raj has a unique way of thinking. It all centers on his ability to simplify a problem to its essence and then, step by step, methodically finding a solution. Raj is also a great teacher by example with an unrelenting focus on finding better ways to under-stand the customer and improve overall business operations. He has always been particularly proud of his team and the culture that he has encouraged. Raj and his team are focused on making the business world a better place.

Ram has spent decades providing thought leadership, counsel, and a perspective few can offer to CEOs and Boards. In today's ever-changing and competitive world, Ram has an innate and prescient way of under-standing changing economic conditions and industry challenges. Not only can he pull together a broad set of data and analysis, but he can also develop actional insights that help companies shift strategies and grow. His intuition and advice help CEOs meet the challenges they face from traditional competitors and industry disruptors. Ram has this ability across many sectors on a global basis.

Raj and Ram are both proponents and teachers of placing digital at the core of any business and how a competitive advantage can result from an integrated set of capabilities. These capabilities focus on the customer and ultimately result in significant, profitable growth for the business. This is not your traditional business book with specific formulas for success. It tackles problems and challenges through the lens of a digital strategy while providing ideas for growth, leadership, and improved customer satisfaction. This book outlines the direction of how a digital business can be applied to create the future. Raj and Ram together help us see the future of business opportunities through their eyes. Both are strong believers that it is essential for any business to develop and implement a digital strategy or die.

Jacques Nasser AC

INTRODUCTION

MANY ORGANIZATIONS TODAY ARE IN THE MIDST OF DIGITAL transformations, investing in a host of technologies as they aim to update legacy infrastructures in order to compete more effectively in highly challenging environments. These are admirable efforts to digitize virtually every aspect of operations. Digital transformation is so important, in fact, that any company declining to move in this direction is a likely, big strategic mistake.

How many of these organizations in the midst of digital transformations are striving to become a true digital business, however? Moreover, how many know what it means to be a digital business? There are similarities as well as differences between digital transformation and digital business, and it is important that business and technology leaders realize this and aim to achieve both.

Digital transformation is mainly internalized and focused on scale and technology investments, with results taking place on an incremental basis. This is achieved by creating a self-service business digital ecosystem rationalizing and leveraging the current technology landscape for the business to collaborate end to end and achieve their outcomes through data, innovation, and with a product engineering approach. Digital business is focused on outcomes and speed and is designed to drive the business growth and market share that are central to all CEOs, boards, and companies.

There is confusion as to what is meant by digital business and digital transformation. From a similarity standpoint, both are ultimately focused on growth, speed, an agile culture, and continuous innovation. And for both, it is important that business leaders take ownership of the initiative to ensure that their organizations identify specific outcomes.

While becoming a digital business across the enterprise is the strategy and goal, many companies do not start their digital business efforts until they complete their company-wide digital transformation. This is a mistake, as companies can move quickly by focusing on specific, bite-sized opportunities while the broader digital transformation is underway.

The main difference between the two concepts is the speed in realizing outcomes and the shift to an agile engineering culture. Digital business accelerates substantive outcomes such as revenue growth, increased market share, and improved operational efficiencies that result in lower costs.

Companies that adopt digital business can potentially realize fast outcomes, be more profitable, and create a competitive advantage in their markets. A digital business leverages technology solutions and data to transform and create a new business model that is more agile and responsive to change.

Given the speed and agility associated with a digital business, it can stand on its own and is not dependent on the digital transformation of any specific business. It is not a one-time transformation, but a new and lasting model that creates unlimited opportunities for growth.

This is not to say digital transformation lacks value. But leaders need to understand that those initiatives tend to be more complex, take longer to implement, are ultimately more costly, and can have a higher risk of disruption to the business. And they also need to be aware that many organizations take a "big bang," end-to-end approach and place a significant emphasis on technology, with little involvement or ownership from the business side.

Rather than focusing on business outcomes, many organizations prioritize doing "something" digitally. These efforts often do not achieve business value, however.

Digital business is about producing effective outcomes quickly and incrementally, where business leaders take the key role establishing measurable outcomes. It is focused on establishing an end-to-end collaborative environment for business, IT, and engineering, and leveraging current technology to create scalable solutions.

For a growing number of organizations, the way forward will be to embrace digital business while also working toward a digital transformation.

Digital business encompasses two main scenarios. One includes cases in which organizations have made initial investments in digital business but have an opportunity to make more significant investments. The other includes organizations that have made significant investments in digital transformation and have been doing so for some time, but can still do more to implement a digital business.

There are several key attributes and components of digital business. One is simplification. Organizations need to undertake business simplification in three key areas of the business: process, product, and data.

Process simplification is an effort to reduce the complexity of business processes across the organization, including all functional units such as operations, accounting and finance, human resources, IT and others. Product simplification reduces the overall complexity of products and services by decreasing the complexity involved in making and managing them. And data simplification aims to eliminate the rigidity and complexity of how data is created, stored, and used in an organization.

Hand in hand with simplification is agility. Developing an agile environment is key to effectively managing changes a company faces or brings on, such as improving product time-to-market, increasing margins and revenue, and reducing cost related to the engineering ecosystem.

Agile organizations are characterized as a network of teams operating in rapid learning and decision-making cycles. The teams instill a common purpose and leverage delivery tools and metadata to provide decision rights to the teams closest to the information. An agile organization ideally combines velocity and adaptability with stability and efficiency.

Another key component of digital business is single source of truth (SSOT), which is the central enterprise data repository of an organization. It provides the organization with a singular and comprehensive view of the business and its customers and helps the organization communicate about data in a ubiquitous language using specific common data points.

The SSOT also provides the ability for companies to be proactive and drive growth across sales, marketing, pricing, and operations. With SSOT, there are no duplicate data entries or version control issues; decision makers receive the right data at the right time; organizations can substantially reduce the time spent on identifying which recorded data is correct; and teams can iteratively improve the data intelligence capabilities of the company.

Yet another component is innovation and experimentation, the ability to create new business models for growth in a speedy and cost-effective way. Within the context of digital business, innovation and experimentation means creating next-generation digital strategies and newer business models and channels, as well as unlocking efficiency gains that are enabled by digital technologies.

From a technology solution perspective, organizations need a robust, open, self-service digital platform to make digital business a reality. Such a platform drives all the technology initiatives and lets business and technology teams collaborate effectively to build digital and data products. The platform centralizes business operations, data management, and workflow management, to deliver an SSOT and drive business insights.

Organizations have multiple options when switching from a conventional operational approach to a self-service platform. These include building the self-service platform in-house; subscribing to specialized self-service platforms for each capability and integrating them separately; and subscribing to one end-to-end self-service digital platform that takes care of all capabilities.

While each organization must choose the best option depending on its internal skillset, budgets, and overall business and digital strategy, for most companies the third option is likely to be the best. It provides one comprehensive platform to drive all digital business initiatives; enables true collaboration among teams; and allows teams to focus on innovation without worrying about technology complexities.

Once an organization has selected and deployed a self-service digital platform, it is time to operationalize digital business across the enterprise. And to truly operationalize digital business, leaders must address four key areas: people/process, data, technology, and sponsorship.

Transforming into a truly digital business means changing the way organizations conduct many day-to-day processes and operations. It can be a difficult journey that requires hard work and is not without risk. But it is necessary in order to remain competitive and thrive in today's business world.

This book serves as a guide for any organization looking to excel at digital business, each chapter covers a different aspect of digital business. One of its most powerful and compelling features is the inclusion of case studies found in each chapter, real examples of how some of the world's largest and most influential companies are succeeding with digital business.

These case studies provide inspiration for any organization looking to achieve success with digital business.

It is important to remember that companies need not go it alone when transitioning to digital business. Many will face challenges shifting to a digital business mindset and culture, which can impede their growth. They struggle with the execution of this approach because they lack practitioners who can solve business challenges with an end-to-end perspective, or because they cannot develop an agile culture for product engineering teams; or because they lack the ability to create an SSOT that enables simplification and experimentation.

The solution is to find a strategic partner that will utilize practitioners and product engineering teams within an agile culture. Such a partner can also help build a culture by finding the right talent and empowering people to succeed. Over time, working with its strategic partner a company can create scale and implement a digital business plan to drive substantive change and sustainable growth for years to come.

Chapter 1

DIGITAL BUSINESS

THE TERMS "DIGITAL BUSINESS" AND "DIGITAL TRANSFORMA-
TION" are frequently used interchangeably. The fact is, although they
overlap and have similarities, they are actually different.

Let us look at the similarities first. Both are focused on growth, speed,
an agile culture, and continuous innovation. And with both, rather than
taking a "big bang" approach, it is more effective for organizations to
start on an incremental basis that does not require a major investment.

For both digital business and digital transformation, it is important
that business leadership take ownership of the initiative to ensure that
specific outcomes are identified. This approach, in conjunction with a
collaborative culture between the business and technology, can deliver
outcomes with speed and minimal disruption to the business.

The key difference between digital business and digital transformation is the speed in realizing outcomes and a shift to an agile engineering culture. Digital business accelerates substantive outcomes that can include revenue growth, increased market share, greater

> "This approach, in conjunction with a collaborative culture between business and technology, can deliver outcomes with speed and minimal disruption to the business."

cashflow, and improved operational efficiencies that result in a lower cost structure.

Companies that adopt digital business potentially can realize outcomes faster, be more profitable, and create a competitive advantage in the market. A digital business leverages technology and data to transform and create a new business model that is more agile and responsive to change. A digital business could be a completely new product or line of business, or it could be a significant change to an existing business line.

> "Companies that adopt digital business can potentially realize outcomes faster, be more profitable, and create a competitive advantage in the market."

As a business consultancy McKinsey & Co. has noted, "Enterprise agility was desirable and is now becoming essential. Agility across a whole enterprise combines speed and stability; helps role clarity, innovation, and operational discipline; and can produce positive outcomes for organizational health and performance."

Because of the speed and agility associated with a digital business, it can stand on its own and is not dependent on the digital transformation of any specific business. Rather than a one-time transformation, this is a new and lasting model that creates unlimited opportunities for growth.

On the other hand, digital transformation is the process of implementing digital initiatives and a combination of tools—primarily systems and data—to facilitate better performance of an existing business. This may include more efficient processes, enhanced customer experiences, and encouraging a more collaborative internal culture.

These initiatives tend to be more complex, take longer to implement, are more costly, and can have a higher risk of disruption to the business. Here is a summary of how the two approaches differ:

Digital Business	Digital Transformation
Focused on business outcomes for growth and continuous innovation with limitless possibilities	Focused on significant transformation in terms of talent, culture, and technology
Business takes ownership and collaborates with technology	Technology drives change and implementation
Incremental approach leveraging existing resources to achieve bite-sized outcomes	A broad-scale approach with a longer timeframe to realize outcomes
Leverages data intelligently to make smarter decisions	Focused on technologies and solutions that require a long-term horizon
Takes the product engineering approach, creating reusable digital assets	Takes an application-based approach that adds a layer of complexity
Focused on simplification and collaboration	Focused at business unit level impedes collaboration
Begins to deliver results within weeks	Takes a longer time to achieve results
Continuous innovation and experimentation at speed with low investment	Innovation requires heavy investment

Unfortunately, many organizations focus on digital transformation with a big bang approach, take an end-to-end strategy, and place a significant emphasis on technology, with little involvement or ownership from the business side. This tends to lead to more expensive and longer sequential processes, slowing down progress and the realization of results.

Rather than focusing on business outcomes, many organizations prioritize doing "something" digitally. But these efforts often do not achieve business value. This leads to additional apprehension and inertia in making investments in digital business.

Digital business is about producing effective outcomes quickly and incrementally. Business leaders take a leading role establishing measurable outcomes. Equally important, digital business is focused on establishing an end-to-end collaborative environment for business, engineering, and leveraging current technology to create scalable solutions. It does not require the completion of all aspects of transformation and can achieve business objectives without causing disruption to existing processes and technology environments.

> "Digital business is about producing effective outcomes quickly and incrementally."

This is not to say digital transformation lacks value. In fact, depending on the organization's maturity level, a mix of digital business and digital transformation will drive the best results. The strategy is gaining momentum.

Research firm International Data Corp. (IDC), in its 2021 Worldwide Digital Transformation Strategies Executive Sentiment Survey, said the number of companies that has two complete, multifaceted, and comprehensive transformation plans or road maps—one for digital transformation technology investment and one for the business transformation—have increased by 76% since 2019.

Companies that achieve the best outcomes are those that can implement digital business and digital transformation simultaneously. The combination of the two is an optimal mix that embraces simplification and creates an agile engineering culture enabling speed and scale. Additionally, a self-service business digital platform eliminates silos as the individual business units converge to operationalize digital business across the enterprise.

Let us explore two distinct scenarios, which each depend on maturity and investments, to understand how organizations can leverage digital undertakings to achieve business objectives.

> "Companies that achieve the best outcomes are those that can implement digital business and digital transformation simultaneously."

Scenario 1

This includes cases in which organizations have made initiated investments in digital business but have an opportunity to make more significant investments.

Many mid-sized and large enterprises, as well as small and startup businesses, did not commit to digital business initiatives in a significant way due to a perception that it is expensive, takes a long time, and disrupts existing operations. They also lacked the appropriate talent and an agile culture needed for digital business.

The best strategy for a company in this category is to initiate a stand-alone digital business approach, where the business takes ownership. The emphasis is to take an incremental approach to solving problems and achieving specific business outcomes.

Initially, the company can seek the assistance of a digital business solution provider, which can serve as a catalyst and strategic partner in creating a culture of simplification. Together they can break each outcome down into smaller use cases, and facilitate end-to-end collaboration of business and engineering teams to create effective outcomes and decision-making.

Two major components of digital business are:

- Single source of truth (SSOT), focused on addressing current pain points, achieving each business function's objectives, and connecting business functions at an enterprise level.
- Innovation and experimentation, to create new business models for growth in a speedy and cost-effective way.

Overall, digital business necessitates business ownership, simplification, and end-to-end collaboration of business and engineering teams, as well as a self-service business digital platform (BDP). This enables an end-to-end collaborative environment, leveraging the latest digital technologies fully automated for high productivity and speed. It is a product approach to creating and consuming reusable digital assets of product components.

Business operations can be centralized to achieve an incremental approach and business outcomes with speed in this self-service BDP rather than the current complex enterprise resource planning (ERP) and other transaction systems.

A self-service BDP for end-to-end orchestration of data, SSOT, and product servicing does not have to transform current transactional systems and platforms. This will reduce investments needed for outcomes.

This end-to-end orchestration of building and launching products spans design, omni-channel experience, data, product engineering, and DevSecOps for security, compliance, release, and site reliability.

Here are examples of how organizations have addressed Scenario 1:

Chocolate Manufacturer Commits to Simplification and SSOT

A manufacturer and seller of premium chocolate has manufacturing facilities across Turkey, the United States, and Europe, and its chocolates are sold all over the world. In the U.S., the company primarily sells through retailers in the food, mass merchandise and drugstores segment, such as Walmart, Target, and CVS; specialty retailers such as Macy's, Bloomingdale, and Barnes & Noble; and warehouses such as Costco.

While the recent Covid-19 crisis brought the company's challenges into sharper focus, it had been clear to the executive leadership even before the pandemic that the company had significant demand–supply synchronization issues.

These issues resulted in:

- Excess inventory in several stock-keeping units (SKUs) that customers did not desire and that soon turned obsolete.
- Severe shortage of best-selling SKUs whose lack of fulfilment resulted in lost sales.
- Periodic manual interventions to facilitate smoother execution of operations in manufacturing, supply chain, and sales functions.

The CEO and the management team subsequently embarked on a fact-finding discovery exercise to understand the current state of challenges and identify a potential roadmap for resolution. The exercise uncovered numerous challenges, including the extensive use of Excel spreadsheets, disconnected and siloed applications, and disparate ways of working.

The use of Excel spreadsheets was a significant deterrent in that the data would often be dated or inaccurate by the time it was leveraged for future decisions. It was clear that the company's limited investments in both building a digital business and enabling digital transformation were inhibiting growth.

The management team subsequently committed to an exercise of simplification by converging the disparate data elements onto a common SSOT platform. It subsequently mandated that all key business decisions be executed based on the data within SSOTs, thereby ensuring consistency.

Subsequently, the SSOT evolved into a strong catalyst that drove a culture of innovation and collaboration across supply chain, manufacturing, and demand forecasting functions. With business taking ownership of outcomes, The company is well on its way to building an effective digital business.

Arnott's Embarks on a Culture of Innovation

Arnott's, in business for more than 150 years, is a leading food brand in Australia with a mission to create delicious products for consumers around the world. Its chocolate, sweet and savory cookies and biscuits are Australia's favorite, with more than half a billion packs consumed each year.

The company's sales and bakery operations are spread across Australia, New Zealand, and Indonesia. Upon undergoing a change in ownership structure in 2020, the new management determined that the business needed to build a digital and analytics mindset in its ways of working.

During its discussions on how to move the business forward, the management team framed two key questions that it wanted answered: Why do shoppers buy our products? And once they do, then what?

Beginning with the end in mind, the management team determined that what Arnott's needed was predictive insights and business outcomes driven by key performance indicators. It subsequently embarked on an exercise to collate data across various applications and systems and automate the onboarding of this data into an SSOT platform.

The intent was to create a strategic data asset that orchestrates and operationalizes consumer insights and business insights that will be leveraged to improve consumer experience while growing bottom-line profitability.

Once the SSOT was developed, Arnott's embarked on a culture of innovation to build incremental insights in the form of bite-sized outcomes to help understand its consumers and business better. With business taking ownership, Arnott's is now establishing the foundation for a digital business.

Global Financial Services Firm Builds a Highly Scalable Architecture that is Flexible and Always Available

The treasury solutions department at a large, global financial services firm was challenged with having to roll out new payment types such as real-time payments (RTP) or instant payments (IP) worldwide in a rapid manner. This was mandated by the central bank regulators of several countries.

The existing payment and channels platform was supporting bulk payments and other bank transfer methods, and the traditional two to three days for transfer was acceptable. But that changed with the new mandate of RTP/IP and growing demand from workers to see money transfer happen instantaneously. This required low latency, high-speed transfers and an always-available architecture.

The firm hired a digital partner to help modernize the payments and channels platform, transforming it from a monolithic architecture to one that is always available, driven by microservices, based on application programming interfaces (APIs), and cloud native. This transformation needed to happen seamlessly, without disrupting current business. The firm had to reengineer the system while the existing types of payments and volume continued to work as before.

The team engineered a set of domains/services and launched these as a new architecture and built a traffic controller to route requests to these new services. The remaining services were supported by the legacy system. This enabled the firm to incrementally move services from the old architecture to a new one.

If at any point in time there were any issues detected with the new microservices, the traffic controller would detect and route traffic back to the old system. This helped harden the new services without disrupting business. Also, the incremental approach made the modernization happen in a seamless way that reduced risk.

The result is a highly scalable architecture that is flexible and always available. The firm was able to implement RTP or IP in multiple countries in a matter of months. Each country implementation has its own regulatory and compliance requirements, and the modern architecture enables the firm to rapidly make needed changes. The implementation was so successful that the firm is applying a similar approach to modernizing its trade, commercial banking, and commercial cards platforms.

How Tesla's Digital Business Focus Helped
to Navigate Chip Shortage

This case study is about how Tesla emerged as one of the auto industry's biggest winners in 2021 where Industry is plagued by semiconductor shortages and snarled global supply chains. Electric-vehicle maker is expected to manufacture 80% more vehicles this year than it did in 2020.

Companies across the globe are trying hard to blunt the damage of the global semiconductor chip shortage to their businesses. But many are overlooking a critical factor that can position their company for a much smoother ride through this turbulent period: the technology/engineering team. They are turning to their engineering team to quickly adjust the way the company designs its products, to mitigate supply chain shocks more rapidly and effectively, with a focus on two key capabilities: designing for resilience and designing for availability.

Global auto industry, hit hard by supply-chain disruptions, is expected to produce around 1% more vehicles than last year and 15% fewer than in 2019 (according to IHS Markit). The chip shortage traces back to late 2020, when demand for vehicles rebounded faster than expected from pandemic lows, catching automakers by surprise.

Tesla adopted digital business practices with highly iterative bite-sized outcomes to quickly rewrite the software necessary to integrate alternative chips into its vehicles to avoid the impact of global shortfall of semiconductors.

- Tesla can design its vehicles from the ground-up, rather than adding parts in a piecemeal fashion over decades as many legacy automakers have done which allowed Tesla to consolidate and integrate systems seamlessly. For example, a distinct group of semiconductors enables features such as speaker control and voice and gesture recognition that in many other vehicles would be controlled separately using more chips. Tesla is benefitted from a highly flexible, adoptable technology platform to make necessary adjustments.

- Tesla's design decouples software from hardware. In a chip shortage, for example, the fewer "hooks" the product has into silicon, the better. When it is not possible to control the hardware, Tesla makes it less critical of the product and increases reliance on software by adding a flexible middleware layer on top of the firmware. Tesla also uses modular design with flexible product architecture wherever possible, including building in additional time to test and qualify multiple acceptable parts.

- Tesla's investments in designing products both for resilience and for availability have paid off during the current chip shortage, and the company's experience demonstrates how the two engineering capabilities can reinforce each other. The electric vehicle maker's decision to use standard semiconductor hardware but to develop in-house the software running on those chips has given the company more flexibility in the components to manufacture its vehicles.

- When it faced a shortage of its typical microcontroller units (MCUs), the company's agile software development capabilities and modular technology architecture helped it rapidly develop and validate 19 new alternative MCUs, while simultaneously developing firmware for new chips made by new suppliers.

- With fewer interdependencies between teams and products, the work required to redesign a single part in the event of a shortage becomes self-contained and less daunting.

- Finally, reducing a product's number of parts and reusing components wherever possible can make the product less susceptible to supply chain hitches.

While traditional automakers often have let parts suppliers handle sourcing chips, Tesla's preference for making vehicle components in-house meant that Tesla had greater supply-chain visibility in some areas, having forged close relationships with semiconductor companies before the crisis began. Tesla, for example, designed the computer that enables its advanced driver-assistance technology in newer vehicles.

The company's small size—and increased demand for electric vehicles—has made it easier to sustain rapid growth. It also gave priority to getting vehicles to customers, even if they are missing a few parts as they could retrofit later.

This is forcing traditional automakers to focus on partnering with semiconductor companies to develop computer chips. Research firm Gartner Inc. forecasts that by 2025, half of the top 10 automakers by market capitalization will be designing at least some of their own chips. It is also motivating for some parts suppliers to do things for Tesla that they are not for other car makers as they want to partner with rising stars who adopted digital platforms faster than the traditional makers.

Most successful companies will become so effective at designing for resilience that they will rarely need to design for availability; if they do, it will be a much faster, smoother process. The result will be companies that are better equipped to handle any supply chain disruption in future.

Scan the QR code to view case-study reference material.

Scenario 2

This scenario includes organizations that have made significant investments in digital transformation and have been doing so for some time but can do still more to implement digital business.

Enterprises can enable digital business by allowing teams to take ownership and not disrupt existing processes. This helps achieve effective business outcomes for faster growth and better investment decisions.

Business should have a say in the transformation roadmap, so that it is implemented incrementally and in line with the business objectives. The transformation roadmap is completed by building solutions iteratively to achieve incremental business outcomes. For digital business, transformation is a means to an end.

To successfully enable digital business, organizations need to consider the following key components:

- Business leaders take ownership and accountability with clear objectives and ways to measure outcomes.
- Practitioners and product owners who understand business and technology can break down pain points into smaller use cases, rather than elaborate requirements. This accelerates decision-making to quickly create new business models.
- Distributed agile digital engineering teams leverage end-to-end collaboration and take an iterative, incremental approach to delivering business outcomes.
- Organizations deploy a BDP for the end-to-end technology environment for the creation and orchestration of digital and data solutions. A BDP integrates into an enterprise's existing digital

ecosystem and automates activities that would otherwise be done manually by software and data engineers. It provides transparency into process bottlenecks and technology issues and ensures discipline by employing industry-leading agile and development processes as well as the collaborative culture required for digital business success.

Simultaneously, enterprises must focus on digital transformation and scale it across the enterprise, to create an end-to-end environment in self-service BDP and orchestration, by rationalizing and leveraging existing technologies including digital technologies. The path to digital technology transformation that creates growth requires taking a business lens coupled with an incrementation approach to eliminate silos and centralizing all operations in this self-service platform rather than each transactional system e.g., ERP. The primary components to accomplish this are:

- Omni-channel experience and engineering consistent across the enterprise for both internal employees and external consumers to engage.
- A data engineering environment to bring data from various sources to create an SSOT, and a data science environment to apply advanced analytics, including artificial intelligence (AI) and machine learning (ML) for predictive and prescriptive analytics for specific analysis and outcomes.
- A product engineering environment that leverages existing digital assets. Both data and product engineering can create and consume reusable assets.
- DevSecOps to establish an end-to-end engineering environment with end-to-end security and compliance to bring about productivity, quality, and reliability.
- Making sure current enterprise standards are incorporated.

Organizations can roll out both digital business and transformation incrementally to create scale by leveraging a BDP and an end-to-end orchestration discipline, to accelerate the transition to an agile culture and continuous innovation.

This will help to ensure end-to-end orchestration internally with scale and speed, without having to make a major investment. This can be accomplished in a short time frame.

Overall, with this approach enterprises can achieve effective business outcomes with speed and transformation of technology at scale with smaller incremental investments. Here are examples of how organizations have addressed Scenario 2:

Novartis Deploys New Platform and SSOT to Eliminate Silos

Novartis is one of the top three pharmaceuticals companies in the world, with a presence in more than 150 countries. In the last few years, Novartis has been betting big on data and heavily leveraging AI and ML to drive its innovation forward. The company wants to leverage the power of data and advanced analytics in a wide range of areas such as drug discovery, manufacturing, drug distribution, clinical trials, finance, human resources analytics, environmental and social governance, and marketing technology.

Central to Novartis' ambitions is its recent push toward creating an enterprise-wide data platform that is completely predicated in the cloud. The idea is to host all the data the company has on the bespoke platform, creating a massive enterprise-wide SSOT and creating useful analytics that can drive innovation.

Over the years, the approach to solving analytical needs was to have each of the business teams create its own sandboxes, which would bring data from myriad sources and then create applications on top. This often meant that there were multiple data platforms, often having the same data in various forms and fashion. Novartis realized that this was creating data silos and leading to inefficient ways to leverage data.

With the new Formula One platform and by creating the SSOT, Novartis aims to have all the data in a single place, thereby eliminating the need for multiple teams to ingest, monitor, and maintain the same data. Instead, teams can focus on innovating based on the data available on the Formula One platform. The company has set up strict governance controls to ensure that data privacy requirements are met, and that only teams and use-cases with the authorization to access the data requested are able to do so.

The platform has been awarded by research firm Gartner for its "Eye on Innovation Awards" in the Life Science category. Based on the platform, Novartis has been able to rapidly onboard use cases such as:

- People & Organization: Finding causal relationships between the culture of the company and its sales performance.
- Operations: Manufacturing analytics focused on real-time identification of issues, with a view to increasing automation on the shop floor with the aid of Internet of Things (IOT)-enabled devices.
- Finance: The ability to predict sales volume and cash flow for the company's drugs—particularly as they go through the cycle of moving from innovative medicine to generics.
- Sustainability: Leveraging data to understand if the goals toward environmentally sustainable practices are being met.
- Further, Novartis is now making this data platform a full-fledged self-service business platform, by rationalizing and leveraging existing technologies and fully automated end-to-end seamless collaboration and speed, consistent across the entire enterprise for scale.

Amazon Focuses on Digital Transformation
and Innovation to Create Value

Amazon is perhaps the best example of a company leveraging digital business to generate significant growth and profitability. The company's success comes from a mix of innovation, agility, and data to launch digital products that deliver exceptional customer experiences.

Amazon did not build this success overnight. It started by selling books online and over time added other products and services such as Amazon Web Services (AWS) Elastic Compute Cloud, Echo, Prime, etc. The company embraces an agile approach focused on being adaptable and moving quickly to fuel growth and expand market share. This corporate dexterity and digital focus are what enable Amazon to quickly launch products and grab substantial market share.

A common thread across Amazon is its relentless use of data to glean insights from the company's operations and customer behavior. This learning culture contributes to developing and delivering products, services, and experiences that solve a customer need.

For example, Amazon uses data to determine where to build fulfillment centers, how to increase productivity across the supply chain, and how to improve demand forecasting by geography and category. Applied to its global operations, data becomes a differentiator in customer experience, leading to better predictive tools and more efficient delivery of shipments, better utilization of trucks, faster fulfillment of orders, and higher margins and profit.

Scan the QR code to view case-study reference material.

Another strength of Amazon's culture is its focus on innovation and experimentation. AWS was the outcome of solving limitations in Amazon's ecommerce book selling business. It has mushroomed into an industry-transforming technology, leveraging AI and ML, to power hundreds of the company's web services. AWS has reinvented the cloud computing concept and made the technology platform accessible to any company on a global scale, earning billions in revenue in the process.

Amazon makes experimentation a core part of its culture, and employees are empowered to explore new ways to add value for customers. For most companies, the fear of failure limits experimentation. But that is not the case at Amazon. Leadership encourages employees to try new things and overcome obstacles. The company is not afraid to create disruptive technology or applications, so long as it leads to better products or services.

The results for Amazon have been impressive. The company's focus on digital transformation and innovation led to phenomenal value creation. Its market cap increased by more than 485% between 2015 and 2020 surpassing $1.8 trillion.

Scan the QR code to view case-study reference material.

Automaker Delivers an Evolving Digital Experience for Customers

An automaker has been building and selling vehicles for more than 100 years. But the company is proof that older businesses can adapt to changing times.

Vehicle lines traditionally have been three to five years, and once a vehicle is delivered there was no change in consumer experience and minimal changes in the vehicle ownership ecosystem.

Consumer expectation of continuously evolving digital experience has extended to their vehicle ownership and commuting, and original equipment manufacturers (OEMs) have to respond to changing consumer expectations.

As a true digital native, Tesla challenged the industry not just in vehicle experience, but also in the buying experience, the way vehicles are powered (charged), and created a process for providing wireless software updates. Consumers and the market alike responded positively to this change.

Unlike Tesla, OEMs including the decades-old automaker did not have a clean state to start. Instead, it had to build on top of complex products, systems, processes, and people already in place. The company embarked on a journey of complex multi-faceted digital transformation. It built a technology foundation and product organization that would support agile culture.

Transforming processes and teams from existing models to a mature Agile, DevOps model takes time. This has significantly increased collaboration between business and technology, and improved time to market. However, it is an expensive process that has to happen over a period of years.

OEMs and suppliers have realized that digitalization does not have to be digital transformation alone. They can execute both digital transformation and digital business in parallel. The company has embraced digital business for its new electric vehicle product lines. With these lines, business and technology are collaborating from inception, and building platforms and solutions in a true agile model that is aligned with the vehicle programs—bringing results to market at a fast pace.

As a result of this approach, the auto manufacturer can deliver an evolving digital experience in vehicles and in the ecosystem. Customer engagement with the company has increased by more than 10-fold over four years, enabling the company to launch data-driven personalized experience. The company is driving millions of charging experiences through its connected charging network via thousands of connected Wallboxes at customer homes and businesses.

Markets, consumers, and critics are embracing this new approach with the company's new products. This agile business model makes the company a true digital player in the automotive space.

Need for a Strategic Partner

Many enterprises face challenges shifting to a digital business mindset and culture, which impedes their growth. They struggle with the execution of this approach for a variety of reasons. These include not having practitioners who can solve business challenges with an end-to-end perspective, difficulty in developing an agile culture for product engineering teams, and the ability to create an SSOT that enables simplification and experimentation.

Many companies are partnering with consulting firms, outsourcers, or technology skills augmentation companies—with limited success. They need a strategic partner that will utilize practitioners and product engineering teams within an agile culture. They can also help to internalize this approach and build a culture by finding the right talent and empowering people to succeed. Over time, companies can create scale and implement a digital business plan to drive substantive change and sustainable growth.

As we have covered in this chapter, companies succeed when they apply a business lens for digital business and transformation. The key ingredient is finding the right talent and building an agile culture with a skilled digital business partner.

Central to this ecosystem is the use of practitioners who can solve any pain point to deliver business outcomes through simplification of end-to-end workflows, collaboration between the business and technology, and the ability break down solutions into smaller bite-sized components. For product engineering teams, this means building agile culture to work in short iterations with practitioners and deliver results at high frequency and speed.

The combination of practitioners, product engineering talent, and a simplified self-service BDP will lead to effective business outcomes. Their output leads to the creation of an SSOT, greater innovation and experimentation, reusable assets, new channels and digital products launched faster and less expensively.

Chapter 2

SIMPLIFICATION AND AGILITY

A KEY COMPONENT OF DIGITAL BUSINESS IS SIMPLIFICATION, which can be achieved outside of the current complex operations and technologies that exist within many organizations.

Over the past several years, we have heard hundreds of business leaders talk about the negative impact of complexity on both productivity and workplace morale. Leaders need to develop the concept of simplification as an imperative and a critical component of their business strategy.

Organizations need to undertake business simplification in three key areas of the business: process, product, and data.

- Process simplification reduces the complexity of processes across the business. This includes all functional units such as operations, accounting and finance, human resources (HR), information technology (IT), etc.
- Product simplification reduces the complexity of products and services by decreasing the complexity of making and managing a product or range of products.
- Data simplification tackles the rigidity and complexity of how data is created, stored, and used in an organization. A key to this is taking an independent approach to developing a single source

of truth to make faster, better decisions—leading to better business outcomes.

To instill a culture of simplification and make simplicity an ongoing capability of your organization, we suggest the following approach.

Business complexity leads to a variety of adverse effects on the organization, stemming from a lack of internal cohesion. This has a negative impact on the efficiency of business operations, due to the lack end-to-end synergies.

It is important to gain a holistic understanding of the business value stream, through the creation of a "heat map" to outline friction points in existing business processes, break down existing silos, and promote a collaborative culture. By enabling end-to-end collaboration, teams will develop a better understanding of what they need to do in order to be successful and shift from a reactive to a proactive approach to solving challenging problems.

The adoption of collaboration tools is essential for developing high-performance teams and business solutions.

Business simplification is a way of thinking rather than a set of action items. It involves continuously simplifying all aspects of the business, be it processes, products, or data management. Shifting the mindset of the organization to embrace simplification takes practice and training to learn the correct methods to effecting change.

> "Business simplification is a way of thinking rather than a set of action items. It involves continuously simplifying all aspects of the business, be it processes, products, or data management."

It is well worth the effort, however, because business simplification is an imperative for sustainable business growth.

Businesses that survive and thrive in highly competitive and rapidly changing environments typically have one thing in common: the ability to be nimble. A successful business is agile; it knows when to bend, pivot, and change to accommodate and adapt to external forces.

Creating an Agile Environment

Developing an agile environment is key to effectively managing the changes a company will face, such as improving new product time-to-market, increasing margins and revenue, and reducing cost related to the engineering ecosystem.

Research firm Allied Market Research has predicted that the U.S. enterprise agile transformation services market will see a compound annual growth rate of 18% between 2018 and 2026. The firm noted that an agile transformation service helps enterprises to sustain intense competition in the market and the threat of market disruption that is driven by advances in technology.

A rise in awareness of agile transformation and a surge in the need to reallocate resources skillfully and rapidly are among the major factors driving the market growth, report said.

Agile organizations are characterized as a network of teams operating in rapid learning and decision-making cycles. They instill a common purpose and leverage delivery tools and metadata to give decision rights to the teams closest to the information. An agile organization ideally combines velocity and adaptability with stability and efficiency.

> "As a catalyst and strategic partner we internalize agile culture for scale and growth driven by our digital business methodology."

The "run-ahead" team creates organizational changes within sprints, just like a development team creates product features within sprints. This team focuses on the highest-priority changes with an agile approach in each sprint, and demonstrates its implementation—when possible—during a sprint review with all stakeholders.

An agile environment facilitates end-to-end collaboration among the business and engineering teams, from ideation to launch. This leads to:

- Alignment on business objectives and predictable business outcomes.
- Higher productivity for engineering teams, with faster feedback loops.
- Embedded quality, security, and reliability throughout the delivery cycle.

- Continuous measurement and improvement of the entire delivery framework.

Organizations with an agile environment focus on delivering high-quality products to clients faster, creating value and a competitive advantage. They can optimize their costs and mitigate risks, by adopting modern delivery frameworks and integrated development workflows, and incorporating consistent and early feedback loops in the delivery cycle.

> "An agile environment facilitates collaboration among the business and engineering teams end-to-end, from ideation to launch."

To progressively expand the agile footprint across an organization, start with the following steps:

- Redefine metrics. Identify measurements for success across the organization for each new scrum team and new product.
- Expand methodically. It can be exciting to produce impressive results, but company-wide improvements require significant process changes. Do not move faster than the organization can handle.
- Create an enterprise-scale DevSecOps platform. Construct engineering practices and principles, developer tools, and elastic infrastructure frameworks that are built to align with the lean delivery models.
- Identify new challenges. Your first agile pilot might have uncovered roadblocks that you did not consider in your original implementation plan. Based on what was learned, update your strategy and maturity roadmap as needed.
- Continue learning. As you roll out new processes, make sure that new team members have the proper training, mentorship, and resources to effectively use agile techniques.

Agile Technical and Business Teams

The concept of Agile software development is advanced and well understood. Now, with the advent of the DevSecOps movement, IT security and operations are also rapidly adopting agility.

Agile is proliferating across other technical domains, such as networking, operations, hardware, and more. DevSecOps fuels agile adoption and enforces the agile principles. DevSecOps is the connective tissue that supports, protects, and gives structure to other elements of the agile environment.

Agile technical teams typically achieve a degree of unprecedented performance and personal satisfaction that comes from better collaboration and a focus on common outcomes.

As the business understands this new way of working, it begins to recognize that the same benefits can be used to create cross-functional agile business teams.

These teams may be involved in any of the functions necessary to support developing and delivering business solutions, including sales, product and corporate marketing, sourcing and supply chain management, operations, legal, procurement, finance, compliance, HR, production, fulfilment, and customer service.

Successful adoption of the simplification mindset and agile frameworks is dependent on having strong executive sponsorship from day one. As we look to change organizational behaviors, activities and processes, executives need to be willing to invest time and budget in re-wiring the culture of the organization.

> "Successful adoption of the simplification mindset and agile frameworks is dependent on having strong executive sponsorship from day one. As we look to change organizational behaviors, activities and processes, executives need to be willing to invest time and budget in re-wiring the culture of the organization."

Top management needs to effectively model the expected behavior by living and breathing the agile mindset, making hard decisions in critical times, and transitioning from a fixed mindset to a growth mindset.

Here are some examples of organizations that are shifting to an environment focused on simplification and agility.

By Breaking Down Problems into Simple Components, Arnott's Realizes Value Incrementally

At snack foods company Arnott's, the key challenge was identifying who the company's customers are and why they buy its products.

Unlike the world of retail, where the retailer knows much about the shopper thanks to the use of loyalty cards at store check-outs or applications that track every step of a customer's online journey, the consumer packaged goods (CPG) market is often constrained by a limited understanding of shopper buying patterns.

In such a scenario, the challenge before the Data & Analytics (DNA) team at Arnott's was to come up with an innovative way to address the problem in such a way that it was more contextual to the CPG business model and not mimic the retail model.

Right at the outset, the DNA team embarked on an exercise of simplification and prioritized key outcomes to understand the customer better. The team decided to derive both consumer insights and business insights in parallel over the next few months.

Consumer insights included aspects such as advanced clustering and segmentation of shoppers, analyzing flavor preferences, understanding product substitution patterns, delving into a competitor's performance, and many more.

Business insights included a detailed analysis of promotion spending, sales analysis by brand categories, a deep dive into production and procurement costs, performance on safety and quality measures, and many more. By adopting a practitioner approach, the team sought to explain shopper behavior through the lens of multiple outcomes.

The result of this bite-sized approach to problem solving was that the problem was broken down into simple components. Building the analytics solution to each of these individual components helped the business also realize value incrementally.

The CXO team assessed the outcomes every month and helped ensure that the organization was prepared to incrementally adapt to the solutions as they were being delivered. With the delivery of one or two outcomes every month, Arnott's was progressively able to develop a better appreciation of its customers and plan its marketing and promotion campaigns with greater accuracy and impact.

**For Consumer Products Company,
Simplification Leads to Digital Business**

When the leadership team at a consumer products company completed a discovery exercise to understand the company's current challenges, it discovered that disparate ways of working and siloed applications and data were the top issues.

These issues in turn resulted in inventory challenges such as excess stock in some SKUs and shortages of others; reduced synchronization between sales, production and supply chain; and limited visibility into real-time order status.

The leadership team at the company determined that rebuilding its technology platform to address all issues at once would be both expensive and time-consuming. The emerging need in the market was agility and speed.

The team determined that the best approach would be to simplify the problem into smaller components, with each component focusing on the realization of a small set of key performance indicators (KPIs). Smaller working groups within sales, production, and logistics were created to focus on the most pressing challenges in their workflow and seek ways to resolve them.

The result of this exercise was the creation of an SSOT data platform, into which data from multiple applications and sub-systems converged. Activities that earlier involved conversations and emails among stakeholders were replaced.

Busines users could directly refer to the SSOT platform for real-time inventory positions, order updates, and forecast consumption patterns. The process of simplification has enabled the company to pivot into a digital business, where technology decisions are underpinned by business outcomes and realizable KPIs.

UWM's Investment in Tech Opens Door to Accelerated Growth and Profit

United Wholesale Mortgage (UWM), a wholesale lender, realized it could create new business growth. But the company did not have the operational capacity or the technology to exploit the market opportunity.

Chairman, president, and CEO Mat Ishbia knew the way to increase market share and deliver industry-best customer service was by investing in technology. His goal was to provide customers with the fastest turnaround time, the lowest rates, and the most convenient way to obtain a mortgage.

The company's investment in proprietary technology was designed to give its broker partners increased productivity and faster transaction processing. Examples include Blink+, a tool that lets brokers take online mortgage applications 24 hours a day; UWM InTouch, a mobile app that allows brokers to manage their loans from their phone; and Brand 360, a multi-functional marketing tool that makes it easy for brokers to market themselves to potential borrowers and real estate agents.

Scan the QR code to view case-study reference material.

These innovative products and services opened the door to accelerated growth and profit.

This technology-led strategy enabled UWM to decrease the average loan processing time for closing mortgages from as much as 60 days to just 17 days. The company has built a team of 1,100 technology employees who are innovating the lending process with new ways to use artificial intelligence, document recognition, and automated workflows.

The company continues to invest in digital solutions to create better customer service delivery. And the results have been impressive. UWM has been the number one wholesale lender in the country for six consecutive years, with a 20% market share. In the first quarter of 2021, the company's net income was up to $860 million compared with $20.3 million in the first quarter of 2020, a 4,136% increase.

In the same period, mortgage origination volume was up 16% to more than $49.1 billion. The company finished the quarter with more than $1.6 billion in cash, which UVM plans to reinvest into digital solutions to continue its growth trajectory.

Scan the QR code to view case-study reference material.

At a Global Financial Services Firm, Agile Teams Align on Business Goals and Deliver Outcomes

At one leading financial services firm, the key challenge was figuring out how to do deliver high-quality products with more predictability and frequency. Unlike startup organizations that have dynamic engineering environments with low-friction points throughout the delivery model, large organizations have complex organizational structure, long-standing ways of working, and multi-faceted dependencies.

In this complex environment, the firm needed to refine how business, technology, and operations teams could align on a common business goal and build a culture of trust and transparency.

The firm embarked on an agile transformation that included a shift in mindset, simplification of portfolio management, modernization of

DevSecOps capabilities, and integration of system observability and security practices.

It adopted a scaled agile framework, restructured its agile teams, and transitioned the business portfolio from projects to products. It created a lean agile center of excellence to lead the change management, developing standards and guidelines that independent agile release train teams adopted to streamline the delivery cadence.

Practitioners were embedded into the agile teams to optimize their engineering environments to support a bite-sized delivery approach. By taking this approach, the organization was able to accelerate time to market from semi-annually to on-demand releases.

Agile teams can now align on prioritized business goals every quarter and delivery outcomes every two weeks. They are able to focus more on innovation, with faster feedback loops and full accountability of product features—from ideation to production launch. Business and technology partners are now confident that they can deliver high value, while reducing overall cost of product maintenance.

Li & Fung Breaks Down Processes into Simple Workflows —And Sees Major Outcomes

Li & Fung needed to address the challenges of getting greater insight into cash balances and accounts receivable. The company wanted to implement a solution that would address the needs in the short term and build greater insight into monitoring and managing the business over a longer horizon.

A cross-functional team worked closely with the Order Planning and Vendor Management teams to understand the actual systems used across all front-line groups. End-to-end process workflow maps were developed to provide a greater view into cross-enterprise interaction.

By talking to the frontline employees, operations leads, and line merchandisers who spoke directly to retail and consumer brands, the cross-functional team learned that much of the process was manual and not efficient. The focus on manual activities also resulted in significant staffing expenditure within Li & Fung.

Most important, the company was spending a lot of time and effort in manually reconciling various forms of data needed to accurately place an order. This reconciliation was important to initiate procurement and production activities, and deliver on customer expectations.

The approach the team took was to document processes and break them down into simple workflows or data flows as a way to identify and implement change. This simplification process was a very important method to identify the root cause of the issues that were uncovered.

Based on these findings, the team developed an automated data correction application to address issues associated with manual reconciliation. The solution provided three major outcomes:

1. A reduction in turnaround time for new orders from a few weeks to a few hours.
2. Improved quality of data for the downstream processing, helping reduce the cost of fixing issues as they were identified and fixed early in the cycle.
3. Simplified work streams resulted in a positive employee perspective.

For Altimetrik, Simplification Leads to Benefits for Employees

At Altimetrik, our mission is to accelerate digital transformation and delivery business outcomes while keeping things simple for our employees.

Among the key steps for accomplishing this are to:

- Make all our employee engagements—the entire experience—real-time across different departments of the organization. That way there is no wait time.
- Create a platform that provides an open environment for employees to communicate and collaborate, and thus have the needed information and transparency to perform and grow with the organization.
- Define and design employee engagement workflows that are self-serviceable and that do not need human interaction, thus enabling employees to accomplish things faster and more independently.

One scenario that we identified as needing simplification for our employees was the time between projects.

The approach we needed to take had to be data driven, create a single source of truth, and make the process self-serviceable.

Thus, the whole process of switching between projects was made an employee-driven decision rather than one driven by the organization. We achieved this by making the workflow self-serviceable and removing manual intervention events. We created a single source of truth by integrating systems, thus making it completely data driven.

Employees are now able to:

- View their engagement end date and prepare themselves by upskilling or cross-skilling based on their interest and passion.
- View all the different opportunities available at Altimetrik real-time.
- Understand their business problems, capability requirements, and role details and express their interest in pursuing an opportunity.

This created an experience where employees and the other stakeholders have access to information at their fingertips, and are now more enabling the process than trying to manage it. This helped improve the employee engagement multi-fold, creating a profound impact on the way we simplified the whole scenario.

The biggest key to simplifying is to provide the transparency and make it real-time. Once the approach becomes data driven and real-time, the feeling of inclusivity kicks in, instilling confidence for the individual and creating a win-win scenario.

Simplicity and Agility—Keys to Business Success

Sometimes simple is best. In order to excel at being digital businesses, enterprises need to embrace simplification. That means moving away from complex operations and technologies, which can have a negative impact on productivity and employee morale.

It is up to business leaders to create a culture of simplification within their organizations as part of their business strategies. They can achieve simplification in the key areas of process, product, and data. As noted earlier, this is not a simple change—but in the end it is well worth the effort.

At the same time, companies also need to embrace agility, and they can do this by creating an agile environment so they can more effectively manage the changes they will surely face in the coming months and years.

Agile organizations function as networks of teams that are quick to learn and adapt to change, and they make decisions quickly. By combining velocity, adaptability, stability, and efficiency, agile organizations can meet challenges and succeed in the world of digital business.

Chapter 3

CREATING A
SINGLE SOURCE OF TRUTH

DATA HAS BECOME THE LIFE BLOOD OF ORGANIZATIONS. In the past the ingestion, management, and use of data was fraught with challenges. Even today, many organizations still struggle with data management and the problem is more complex because of the enormous volumes of data they possess.

The struggles include managing data in silos across the enterprise, with a lack of standardization and coordination needed to build a single data repository. What typically results from this type of environment is a partial view into customer insights and an inconsistent approach to customer engagement strategies.

What is missing in this environment is that the business does not really take ownership of data. Also, when it comes to creating an SSOT, many organizations take a "big bang" approach rather than a more thoughtful, incremental one.

> "When it comes to creating a single source of truth, many organizations take a 'big bang' approach rather than a more thoughtful, incremental one."

SSOT, the central enterprise data repository of an organization, provides a company with a singular and comprehensive view of its business and customers. The SSOT provides a business with the ability to be proactive and drive growth across sales, marketing, pricing, and operations.

This helps the organization communicate in a ubiquitous language using specific common data points. Ubiquitous language also helps create a coherent culture and mindset across the organization, and helps break down silos.

As organizations are becoming increasingly agile and adaptive in nature, decision cycles begin to shorten. People make decisions more quickly. This reduction in decision cycles has few challenges, such as the need for real-time information, visibility across the organization, and management of all sources of data including internal, external, structured, and unstructured.

In addition, organizations need to have in place the predictive tools and data models to track and measure outcomes, so they can evolve their strategies and adjust them as needed.

To help organizations drive these shorter decision cycles and keep a long-term focus, the need to manage information is paramount. When this information is spread across the organization in a siloed manner and in different systems, there is a risk of disjointed decisions that can adversely impact customer experience and growth. Data not only helps drive profitable growth, it also improves customer satisfaction, controls costs, and empowers employees.

> "When this information is spread across the organization in a siloed manner and in different systems, there is a risk of disjointed decisions that can adversely impact customer experience and growth."

An SSOT is a means to address these critical issues. It is a process of ingesting all information across the functions, touchpoints, and channels of an organization into a common repository in a systematic and periodic manner.

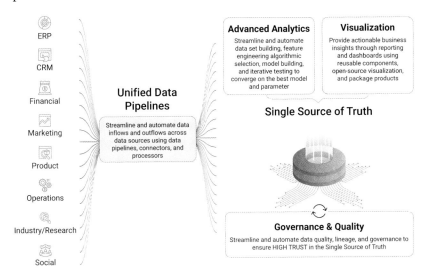

As consulting firm Deloitte has noted, "digital technologies that support multiple flexible methods of working are crucial today, both in the workplace and in the future of work. Having an SSOT is no longer a 'nice to have', but rather a critical way to connect to the experts and critical knowledge within an organization. It can save time and effort by curating valid, reliable, and accurate knowledge."

Among the key benefits of SSOTs:

- No duplicate data entries or version control issues.
- Decision makers receive the right data at the right time.
- Organizations can substantially reduce the time spent on identifying which recorded data is correct.
- Teams can iteratively improve the data intelligence capabilities of the company.

Management consultant, educator, and author Peter Drucker stated that information is "data endowed with relevance and purpose." Siloed data, such as customer retention rates, sales figures, and supply costs, gets more value if it has been integrated with other data and transformed into information that can guide decision-making.

Market share data put into a historical or a competitor context suddenly has meaning. Figures may be climbing or falling relative to benchmarks or in response to a specific strategy or promotion.

One of the keys to a successful SSOT strategy is collation. Many organizations have invested in large to medium ERP platforms and consider them to be the backbone systems of their organizations. While this might be true, that does not make ERP an SSOT. These are operational systems that help drive the processes in a coordinated way. The data generated by ERP systems needs to be extracted and brought into a single platform or a database which can then be aligned with other aspects of the organization.

> "SSOT applied to AI and ML tools creates the methodologies and algorithms that drive growth."

The process of bringing data from multiple systems such as ERP, product lifecycle management (PLM), marketing, sales, finance, and management and storing them into a closely related structure is the collation component of SSOT.

The data collation needs to happen in a systematic way. For example, a sales cycle may be tracked on quarterly schedule while a production cycle may be tracked on a weekly schedule and a human resources cycle on a daily basis. The process of understanding different dimensions of the frequency and how the data is created and used, and then standardizing them is part of the systematic process.

This contributes to data standardization and helps create a ubiquitous language in terms of time, material, and quality of what an organization works on.

Perhaps the most important aspect of SSOT is periodicity. How frequently is the data being collated to understand the ongoing changes of the organization? How frequently are insights being generated from the data and how frequently are these insights and data used by the organization? These are extremely important aspects of a viable SSOT.

> "Perhaps the most important aspect of SSOT is periodicity. How frequently is the data being collated to understand the ongoing changes of the organization? How frequently are insights being generated from the data and how frequently are these insights and data used by the organization?"

The graphic below summarizes the concept of an SSOT.

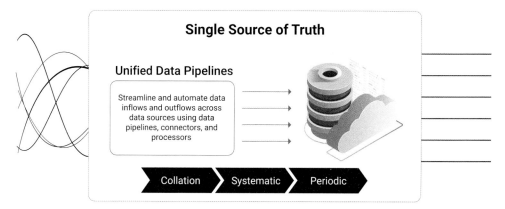

One of our customers, a large financial technology company, successfully took the bite-sized approach, where we broke the solution down into small domains or business units. We identified the SSOT for particular business units, collated data from various sources, standardized the data, and then set the periodic updates of data into the SSOT.

For example, the first business unit we focused on was the customer team and a customer SSOT was created, in parallel with a product SSOT that we also created. The objective was to establish smaller, more focused SSOTs that will eventually roll up into a central SSOT without disrupting the current business.

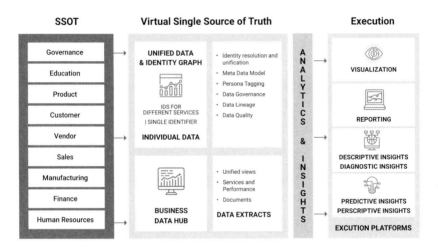

The concept of SSOT across the organization was then achieved by the virtual database created by data federation, which does not contain the data itself. Instead, it contains meta data that describes the actual data, including its location. Other instances of the data refer to the main SSOT location, so that updates to the data in the primary location are spread to the entire system and the likelihood of duplicate values is eliminated.

This then became the enterprise-level view, and increased the velocity of decision-making in the organization.

It is important to understand that there are SSOT systems, and they are quite different from the SSOT itself. These are operational systems that are needed to drive many business platforms such as ERP or PLM.

The SSOT itself is beyond the systems; it is all about the actual data and the insights that can be derived from SSOT. One of the leading automotive manufacturers understood this early on, and created a strategic roadmap for its SSOT for vehicle, consumer, and product lines.

The data from its multitude of ERPs, PLMs, and custom applications were brought into a single data platform. The differentiation of operational systems and the data of the operational systems was understood, and this helps the company today in using this centralized data to drive many customer-focused engagements across the product and vehicle lifecycles.

One of the paths to success for some organizations developing an SSOT is to set up a clear collation, have a systematic and periodic framework in place, and standardize the framework for the organization. This does not impact any active business and a platform is built around the business to support the framework.

Once the platform and framework are set, individual business functions and business outcomes are identified and migrated to this platform, which helps drive SSOT. This is an approach taken by leading pharmaceutical companies, and is one that can support organizations that need to adopt SSOTs.

Another example, a global auto manufacturer/supplier underwent several mergers and acquisitions across the globe that resulted in disjointed data systems, silos, and disparate product masters and charter accounts. At central level, the company struggled to manage data across different ERP, customer relationship management (CRM) and other systems.

The company is undertaking the creation of a central business group to build a standard product master and charter accounts across business functions mapped into each individual group for an SSOT. The approach is to focus on business taking ownership to coordinate and build the business unit SSOTs. The company decided to create account/product masters for sales, production, supply chain, etc., and enable finance to tap into them.

Information from various sources will be brought into a Business Digital Platform to leverage product and account masters, so the data can be consolidated into an enterprise SSOT. Each group's business team will have full ownership and work in collaboration with engineering teams in a true agile approach. The goal is to create a culture of collaboration and iterative processes to converge data into an SSOT, to make better decisions without disrupting current business.

Among the best practices for operating an SSOT are:

1. Separate processing and storage engines in the architecture, which helps in expanding either based on the need, without contention.
2. Unify security, governance, and metadata management, which helps to not only protect data but also to optimize workload performance, eliminate resource content, and ensure consistency.
3. Deploy a cloud data platform that supports data loading and analytics on mixed data formats, with complete transactional integrity and transferability.
4. Emphasize encryption, access control, and other targeted protocols within an overall cybersecurity architecture.
5. Evaluate the data migration strategy on a regular basis to cater to business needs and in case of a data breach or ransomware attack.

Many organizations achieve the power of SSOTs by driving business insights and integrating all the data from enterprise systems to a single repository.

The SSOT as a concept is quite relevant in a self-service business digital platform, as it serves as a central point from which the business outcomes can be built and delivered to customers. A self-service business digital platform is a multi-purpose hub that helps an organization coordinate work and support business interactions between people and technology.

Organizations that have a large IT infrastructure may struggle to integrate different systems, costing valuable time and resources. This is addressed by centralizing business operations and creating a self-service platform that leverages current digital technology.

It is the intelligent integration and orchestration of different digitalization technologies into a single solution (or solution stack) that enables the technologies to create new digital business assets.

A self-service business digital platform will help build an SSOT for an organization in an efficient way, by helping to align to the principles of collation, systemic and periodic. The patterns of data ingestions, storage, and processing are part of a self-service business digital platform, and reusing them will help standardize the approach and accelerate the development process.

Here are a few examples of how companies are successfully leveraging SSOTs.

Following Acquisition, Novartis Creates SSOT
and Delivers Significant Business Value

Following the acquisition of Advanced Accelerator Applications (AAA), a France-based pharmaceuticals group, it was imperative for Novartis to bring AAA's data into its ecosystem.

As with any acquisition, the challenge was that the two different companies had different IT systems and analytics platforms. AAA's data was in different places and formats, and it was a labor-intensive process to extract this information. This made data analysis slow, cumbersome, and complicated to scale up. Manual and potentially error-prone reports had to be drawn particularly because of the myriad and disparate set of IT systems that the two entities had.

The AAA program was initiated to build a data lake with all the relevant data from various functions such as commercial, finance, technology operations, etc. into Novartis' enterprise-wide data platform. This has now become the SSOT for all AAA data from which the AAA and Novartis teams alike could build insights through custom dashboards, self-service business intelligence (BI) tools, and data APIs.

The upshot of this was that for the first time, business and IT teams from both entities were able to look at the same data and draw insights from it for their demand planning, forecasting, and field activity reporting. This reduced the reporting time from days to a couple of hours. Also, since this was built on an SSOT, there was an enhanced element of trust on the results from the business team.

This has resulted in significant business value.

Automaker Improves Customer Experience and Product Launch Cycle Time

Automakers over the years have created multiple data warehouses and data marts that were focused on specific regions and business functions. Connecting the dots across the enterprise and being able to analyze the data sets and monetize them involves significant time and cost without SSOTs.

One such company created a consistent approach to land, process, and make data available for analytics and products regardless of sources and tools. The data processing is managed across three major zones.

As data is integrated and processed, based on business needs, it is analyzed via transit leveraging stream analyses to predict next best action or stored and processed for advanced analytics.

This approach enables the company to enrich data and make it readily available to solve business problems within a short turnaround time. The automaker is able to integrate customer data from disparate data sources (CRM systems, sales, service, etc.) into a data lake and process data to connect the identity of customers and households.

Data pipelines ingest and process connected and non-connected vehicle data on a daily and real-time basis, and machine learning models analyze and predict failures of auto parts.

With the upgrade, the company was able to improve customer experience and engagement by having a 360-degree view of customers across all lines of business, including vehicle ownership, service, credit, scooter rental, etc. It will reduce lead times to analyze parts failures and fix issues, reducing recall costs in new vehicle lines.

Total cycle time for defect failure analysis will drop from six months to three weeks, resulting in tens of millions of dollars in cost savings. An additional benefit comes from a 23% improvement in product launch cycle time, which reduces costs by more than 20%.

Arnott's SSOT Facilitates Faster Decision-Making

Arnott's realized that achieving business outcomes at high velocity would require a seamless synthesis of disparate data elements across siloed business applications. But communication among these applications in many instances was not in real time.

For example, if the business team required an understanding of how monthly sales performance was influenced by trade promotion spending, users had to manually extract information from multiple applications and perform correlations.

The data team at Arnott's embarked on an exercise of building an SSOT platform that would converge data from both internal applications and external data entities. The frequency of data aggregation was near real-time, thereby removing any information "gaps" that would creep in during delays.

The aggregated data was subsequently cleansed, standardized, and enriched on the SSOT platform, so that insights could be easily extracted from the homogenized data set.

An SSOT has the potential to enable Arnott's to take up newer business use cases and provide quicker business insights. It facilitates faster decision-making and reduces challenges that arise due to disparate data sets.

Large Manufacturing Company Leverages SSOT to Make Better Decisions and Accelerate Innovation

A large manufacturing trading company had more than a dozen data sources containing similar supplier information, such as name and address. But the content was slightly different in each source. For example, one source identified a supplier as ABC; another called it Abc, Inc. and a third labeled it ABC Corp.

This inconsistency in the data attributes created multiple challenges from a planning and reporting aspect. Missing was a master data or a centralized data repository storing the information in a consistent way.

As there can be multiple SSOTs at the business-unit level, it is important that they are managed at that level to avoid redundancy. No two SSOTs can both be the master for the same business of an organization. For example, a product master can be owned by the product team and a customer master by the customer team, but there should not be another product master maintained and managed by the manufacturing team.

There are times when business function SSOTs across the organization can be collated and synchronized from an enterprise-level SSOT. To accomplish this, the company took a bite-sized approach to expand adoption across people and processes in an agile manner.

Using Fuzzy logic and artificial intelligence, the company was able to sift through such data inconsistencies and variations to assemble an SSOT. This not only helped to drive consistent reporting, but also uncovered many redundant activities being performed across the enterprise. It also helped to reduce the cost of planning and financial overhead as the SSOT from the vendors/suppliers made managing information more efficient.

Having an enterprise-level SSOT enables the company to make better decisions and accelerate innovation and experimentation to build digital products.

Altimetrik Builds Employee Engagement Around SSOT

One of the biggest challenges we faced at Altimetrik with respect to employee engagement was data spread across multiple systems and not synchronized. This made it difficult to provide a consistent and unified experience to our employees.

The only way to address the problem was to create an SSOT for all of the employee data and build the engagement experience around that.

There are multiple facets and paradigms when it comes to segmenting employee data in an organization, and we are not talking about getting all that into a single system. Data was the key to making the whole engagement experience real-time and simplified. And to create that experience, it was mandatory that there be an SSOT.

As part of the solution, we finalized on multiple SSOTs based on performance management, opportunity identification and onboarding, innovation, etc. And we created our workflows and interaction design based on these SSOTs and the data attributes to deliver the real-time goal.

SSOT: The Key to Optimizing Data Value

Data is one of the most valuable assets a business possesses today. But if that data is not leveraged in the right ways its value can diminish—and it can even become a liability. Many organizations continue to struggle with data management, in part because so much information is coming into their systems and from so many different sources.

Creating an SSOT is a way to ensure that data is up to date and accurate for all users throughout the organization. To build this SSOT, companies must take a thoughtful and incremental approach rather than attempting to do it overnight.

If it is built correctly, the SSOT becomes the central data repository for the entire organization, delivering a singular and comprehensive view of the business and its customers. The SSOT enables businesses to be proactive and drive growth across all aspects of their operations.

Chapter 4

INNOVATION
AND EXPERIMENTATION

IN THIS AGE OF DIGITAL BUSINESS, ORGANIZATIONS ACROSS ALL industries are in the midst of fundamental transformations. Such transformations do not guarantee success, however. Only those organizations that are reimagining their business around digital innovation and open to experimentation can achieve sustainable growth and enhanced margins. Only they will be able to thrive through disruption. Others will be left behind; or worse, they will be wiped out.

Global consulting firm Boston Consulting Group, which presents an annual ranking of the world's 50 most innovative companies, noted that "innovation is essential. Nearly 75% of companies say innovation is one of their top three management priorities, and 35% rank it above all others. That is not surprising. After all, a winning innovation strategy—paired with the right innovation system—can make a big difference."

Companies need to take a holistic approach to digital innovation and experimentation, including product innovation, process innovation, and experience innovation. In all three cases technology is driving the innovation.

> "Companies need to take a holistic approach to digital innovation and experimentation, including product innovation, process innovation, and experience innovation. In all three cases technology is driving the innovation."

By digital innovation, we mean creating next-generation digital strategies and newer business models and channels, and unlocking radical efficiency gains that are enabled by digital technologies. This is easier said than done. Enterprises need a highly structured framework and systematic approach to championing innovation and gaining sustainable competitive advantage.

To stay ahead of competitors, you must innovate quickly to cater to changing market needs. This means you must fail fast, innovate fast and scale fast. Keep ideating, prototyping, and commercializing your ideas.

It is a continuous process of looking for opportunities to transform the way we live our lives and enterprises do business. In today's technology-driven commercial landscape, you want to achieve faster time to value with better customer experience and cost-effective business operations. You need innovative business models, processes, tools, and technologies to commercialize your ideas quicker and better.

Innovation is the fundamental essence of a business, not an ad-hoc assignment. Therefore, it is important to treat innovation as an integral part of a business strategy. And to achieve this as an organization, you need to foster a culture of innovation and a powerful ecosystem.

So, how should you create an enterprise environment that will inspire extraordinary contribution from people brimming with imagination, initiatives, and passion? Here is a framework to help you set up a process, a system, and a routine to make innovation your business-as-usual.

> "Innovation is the fundamental essence of a business. It is not an ad-hoc assignment."

The Innovation Playbook

The four pillars of innovation are:

Digital Culture

Talent

Innovation Platform

Governance

Digital Culture

In today's digital world, what you need is a work environment that not only embraces digital culture from the top on down, but also ensures that employees are empowered to cultivate a completely digital mindset. The leadership vision and goals need to be aligned with this culture and fostered accordingly. There must be an open culture that embraces collaboration and communication which results in increased productivity and innovation.

Talent

You need to hire the best talent. But it does not stop with hiring. You must keep teams motivated and engaged, and nurture the talent to meet the organization's innovation agenda. Mentorship programs; memberships in forums where people can present ideas; and participation in TechTalks and conferences are all required to boost innovation.

Along with this, organizations need to provide the required training or make training resources available as necessary. And of course, you must reward and recognize innovative endeavors by employees as appropriately. This not only emphasizes the importance of innovation to the organization, but can also help retain top talent as well. Perhaps most important, give people challenging work, where their ideas and learnings can be put to real business benefit and enable continuous learning.

Innovation Platform

An innovation platform is more of a complete innovation ecosystem with an end-to-end flow to manage ideas. To start with, you need an "idea bank" that serves as a source of ideas from individuals, as well as real business scenarios and input from market research. Next, you need an innovation committee that can review the ideas at multiple levels, shortlist the best ones for prototyping, and check the business viability and possible productization.

> "Altimetrik's approach is to quickly and inexpensively develop a proof of concept through a self-service business digital platform."

Collaboration among innovators is key to bringing like-minded people together, creating groups, and providing upskilling programs based on skill gaps. Once you have decided which ideas to take up for prototyping, the next most important aspect is the availability of technology tools and "innovation sandbox" environments for rapid prototyping.

Managing intellectual property is of paramount importance in today's highly competitive digital environment. Identifying ideas that are suitable for filing patents and providing complete guidance on patent filing is part of this process. Motivating individuals to come up with ideas worth patenting can only be achieved through appropriate rewards and recognition.

Governance

The whole innovation program must be governed in the best interest of the business at large, helping to improve it and unlocking new opportunities to enable faster growth. Start with big, bold business goals with small milestones. Conducting weekly, monthly and quarterly reviews to validate that the program aligns with the organization's vision, goals, and expectations is mandatory.

Setting measurable key performance indicators for leadership teams and cascading them to the individual level helps keep all activities on track and aligned.

Innovation is a continuous process of improvement for commercial benefits. In a pleasantly flat hierarchy, where innovative ideas are well received across the organization, the journey of innovation involves six important phases as displayed in the following diagram:

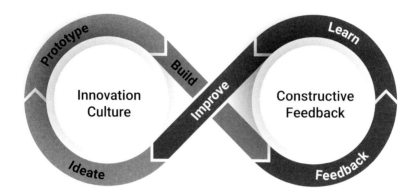

A great idea should be executed, and its prototype should be created with an intention to trial the business potential of that idea. If the prototype stands up to the industry standards and regulatory norms, it must be pushed for productization.

The product should be commercialized if it passes all the quality assurance tests. If it does not, leaders should provide constructive feedback to the innovators and developers of the product. This feedback should encourage the innovators to make improvements, perhaps offering new ideas.

This is what an innovation culture makes possible. People having different talents come together, build innovative business models together, fail together, learn together, and ultimately develop something extraordinary that transforms the world.

Prioritization Matrix for Innovation

Innovation involves effort that results in business impact. There are easy-to-implement and difficult-to-implement innovation activities that can have varying degrees of business impact. Which quadrant of the Implementation v. Impact space your organization falls into depends on:

- The end results you want to achieve
- The resources you have
- The culture of your organization

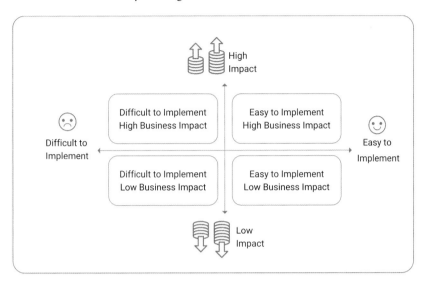

A Formula for Successful Innovation

Here is a brief guideline for how to drive an innovation agenda effectively and create a sustainable competitive advantage.

Ingenuity: Create a bank of ingenuity of ideas that have the promise of disrupting the status quo. Do not discard them, even if they seem impossible, without thoughtful consideration. This is where innovation starts.

Necessity: Prioritize the business functions that have the maximum need.

Nimble: Agility is the key.

Outside in: Put customers and external stakeholders at the center of innovation while you design the innovation program. Make customer value creation and experience top priorities as you put your strategies and action plan into play.

Vision: One of the most important parts of innovation is to set the vision and goals with expected metrics, and have alignment among all stakeholders. Leadership must inspire the organization with appropriate actions, rewards, and recognition.

Automate: Automate as much as possible. Let the team focus on core action items while automation takes care of non-core items.

Trial: Deploy controlled trials, or pilot programs, to demonstrate the value. Fail fast, learn fast, and scale fast.

Iterate: Based on the trial outcome, keep iterating until you perfect the implementation. Make bite-sized iterations. Do not get stuck waiting for the big bang approach.

Optimism: Create talent and user outreach programs to generate constant optimism in the innovation organization. This is one of the most important facets of innovation-driven strategies.

Navigate: The digital innovation leaders must navigate teams to stay focused on the right business outcomes, and they must work to cut out distractions. The innovation journey will be difficult, but it will be worthwhile as the first signs of success set in.

Here are several examples of organizations that are excelling at innovation.

Fintech Firm Turns Innovation into Improved Direct Marketing Performance, Resulting in Higher Revenues

This fintech company's business model was highly reliant on data and analytics. The challenge was that it was getting data from various sources and did not have a reliable collation mechanism for the data. Moreover, the data science teams were running their advanced analytics models on local machines. The data matching and pairing process was cumbersome, and therefore the teams typically built models with a frequency of one every five months. Even the basic uses of this data—for example, list management or basic analysis—were unnecessarily manual, complex, and error prone.

The firm hired a digital business partner to put an appropriate solution in place. The partner applied the principles of simplification, SSOT, and innovation to address the challenges.

In terms of simplification, instead of charting a grandiose multi-year program for building a data lake, the partner—along with the company's stakeholders—identified a bare minimum set of data sources, brought their data into a data lake, and built and deployed ML models.

All this was done in a matter of weeks. In the next iteration, more data sources were brought in, the existing ML model was enhanced, and new ML models and use cases were built and deployed to production.

And to ensure faster time to value, the entire architecture was built on the cloud, using managed services.

All the while, the team ensured that the incremental data lake was kept pristine, well governed, and high quality. It was not just a matter of building it as an SSOT, but also retaining it as such.

Under the digital business philosophy, innovation is not just about creating new things and processes, but also embracing and adopting relevant innovations in building solutions to business problems. In keeping with that philosophy, the partner embraced the cloud innovation paradigm, along with implementing a smaller chain of innovations specific to the data and context of this fintech company.

Both the fintech company and its digital business partner were clear from the start that any task that did not directly and immediately lead to a business output would be cut down.

For example, both parties agreed that documentation would be kept to the bare minimum. Instead, the engineering team was mainly focused on writing, testing, and deploying code in frequent intervals. The machine learning models created using candidate algorithms such as XGBoost, LGBM, etc. were updated regularly. There was a collaborative cadence established between the key stakeholders of both companies. This agile culture and approach ensured that the business teams at the fintech company got to see frequent and tangible value adds to their business. It was a win-win for all.

Among the results of these efforts were an improvement in the efficiency of direct marketing performance, resulting in higher revenues; an approximately 80% reduction in new model development timelines; an increase in the number of useful ML models built and deployed in a short period of time; and an increase in the overall positive energy in the company, created by the quick value generation of these initiatives.

United Wholesale Mortgage Drives Innovation to Deliver the Best Tools for Brokers

United Wholesale Mortgage (UWM) has grown to become America's largest wholesale and purchase lender by focusing on innovation and experimentation.

The company has used new and innovative products and services to test their viability and attractiveness with customers. The learnings are used to determine whether a new product or service is viable. If the results do not meet expectations, then there is no hesitation in ending the pilot or program. This philosophy demonstrates that UWM is willing to experiment and learn in order to grow its business.

In September 2021 the company accepted the first-ever cryptocurrency mortgage payments by its borrowers. UWM used these payments as a learning tool to better understand and evaluate how it can scale cryptocurrency payments for its customers.

"We're proud to be the first mortgage lender to successfully pilot this technology and further demonstrate that we're innovating for the long term," said Mat Ishbia, president and CEO of UWM. He went on to conclude that given the incremental costs and regulatory uncertainty of cryptocurrency, the company decided not to proceed beyond the pilot.

Continuous innovation driven by technology is a priority that starts with senior leadership. The company is focused on initiative projects that deliver exceptional customer service and speedier transaction processing for its mortgage brokers and customers.

An example of this is BOLT, a self-service platform that can provide an initial mortgage approval within 15 minutes. Another milestone for the company is its Virtual E-Close service, an industry first, end-to-end digital origination process without the need for a wet signature.

UWM is committed to driving innovation in the pursuit of delivering the best tools for its brokers and a seamless end-to-end digital experience for its customers. Innovation is part of the UWM culture and a key driver of its growth.

Agricultural Logistics Company Leverages Blockchain to Address Supply Chain Challenges

The supply chain and trade finance industries face serious challenges. Globalization has made supply chains significantly more complex, involving multiple players from around the world and a great deal of coordination among large numbers of stakeholders who do not necessarily trust each other.

While this has driven up operating costs, increased regulation is driving up the cost of regulatory compliance. Many processes are outdated and paper-based, and supply chains suffer from a lack of transparency due to data not being readily available.

Traditionally, this industry contains a combination of paper-based processes and digital systems, where information is held up in silos. A lack of end-to-end process integration and information sharing results in problems regarding the tracking and tracing of products.

Tracking and tracing is key to digital supply chains, as changing consumer behavior and market conditions demand higher supply chain visibility. The traditional methods are, however, slow, fragmented, and ineffective. This makes it problematic to validate a product's origin, location, or specific characteristics.

An agricultural supply chain and logistics company is taking innovative steps to address the various challenges. For example, it is leveraging blockchain to address the underlying challenges inherent in collaborating across a distributed, fragmented supply chain ecosystem.

Blockchain is a promising technology for the food manufacturing supply chain and food safety traceability system because of the characteristics involved, such as the irreversible time vector, smart contract, and consensus algorithm.

The technology ensures privacy by providing appropriate visibility. Transactions are secure, authenticated, and verifiable. There is also trust, as transactions are endorsed by relevant participants.

Among the other key business benefits are a reduction of costs and complexity; decreased commercial risk and customer returns; improved quality of merchandise delivered to customers; greater security and immutability; reduction in fraud; error-free processes; automation of commercial processes; accelerated flow of goods; and real-time on-demand access to information.

Stellantis Focuses on Speed and Agility to Create a Radical Shift in Customer Experience

With the advent of digital technology, some businesses are experimenting with their traditional lines of business to explore newer markets or create niche markets to stay relevant, competitive, and profitable.

For example, automotive giant Stellantis is redefining its business models and reassessing revenue growth opportunities centered on digital and data capabilities such as the use of sensors, IoT devices, and the sophistication of vehicle connectivity.

The company's most skilled technology teams are running innovation and experimentation pipelines around promising initiatives to enhance customer experience and drive significant business growth at the same time.

Stellantis plans to move its vehicles from a dedicated electronic architecture to an open software-defined platform to seamlessly integrate with the digital lives of customers. Over-the-air (OTA) updates to add innovative features and services can keep vehicles fresh and exciting, even years after they have been built.

The company will leverage the speed and agility associated with the decoupling of hardware and software update cycles, to create a radical shift in customer experience. To power this transformation, Stellantis estimates it would employ more than 2,400 software engineers by 2024.

While Stellantis has about 12 million monetizable connected cars today, it expects this number to grow to almost 26 million by 2026. The company plans to grow its software and connected services business through services and subscriptions, features on demand, data as a service and fleet services, vehicle pricing and resale value, and service retention and re-selling.

The company is planning to invest €30 billion in software and electrification by 2025. This will fuel top-line growth with a revenue of €4 billion by 2026 and accelerating to €20 billion by 2030.

Altimetrik's Approach to Innovation

Altimetrik has a practitioner-driven approach for Digital Business enablement that is used for partnering with our clients. The role of our practitioners is to elevate the conversation beyond engineering to a broader business perspective to identify the client challenge(s) and to focus on developing a solution to address them. A common element in this process is to focus on innovation and experimentation that will lead to a desired business outcome.

A key element in our approach is leveraging a business digital platform where all stakeholders share a common front-end interaction layer.

Innovation can be divided into 2 distinct parts:

1. A unique approach toward innovation
2. A business digital platform to innovate

Innovation Approach

As noted earlier, innovation starts by being able to clearly define the business challenge and the expected outcome to be delivered. These are the tangible issues that our practitioners tackle while trying to simplify and provide a solution set for digital enablement.

We have also made it easier to detail the business challenge by having templates for the practitioner to identify and define the situation in a more comprehensive way. The innovation process starts with defining a problem statement and capturing ideas across the working team in real time. These are accessible through the platform for review, team members have an opportunity to submit additional suggestions or propose an innovative idea and solution in a collaborative setting.

Each idea is reviewed by an engagement and/or capability center leader and those that are viable move on to the proof of concept (POC) stage. As part of the POC, the technology and data to be utilized is reviewed for viability to deliver the stated outcomes. The teams are given enough sprint cycles to work on the POC and will demonstrate their working demo to the project leads. After review and assessment, the approved solutions are then moved to the next level for deployment.

Innovation Platform:

A key element of implementing innovative solutions is enabled by a platform to ideate, test, and deploy the business solution. This innovation platform provides visibility to all team members throughout the development cycle. In the event of multiple proposals that have been put forth, the team and respective leads can review and choose the most viable solution. The process is collaborative and there is a seamless end-to-end integration across our Digital Employee Engagement platform (DEX) and Lazsa, our Pro-Code PaaS used for proof of concept development.

The DEX platform is available as a mobile application and is downloadable from the App Store or Play Store and is available to all employees. DEX empowers innovation in real time, seamlessly, and is accessible across devices for all employees anywhere and anytime. This is a highly collaborative process in which employees can work across the globe to build innovative solutions. Employees are also able to browse a portfolio of business challenges, interact with the leads, and submit their ideas for solving them.

Once ideas are selected, they are then onboarded to the Lazsa, PaaS platform for development. Lazsa, being a pro-code platform, provides the needed speed and agility for our employees to be laser focused on developing their respective solution and implementation.

The platform provides a seamless and collaborative experience to our employees across the entire innovation lifecycle including team interaction, communications, and team engagement. Innovation is now part of Altimetrik's DNA and is a core competency of our practitioners.

Below are sample innovative solutions from our employees and in our Innovation Library.

1. Test Automation Reporting & Analytics (TARA) – Insights to power Test Automation

Idea Unique Selling Proposition (USP): Bridge the last mile gap between investing and maintaining test automation. Filter False Positives, noise generated by non-code related failures, from execution reports.

Business Challenge: As organizations scale up digital transformation, they need to invest in Test Automation which is feedback to the DevOps pipeline for Continuous and Frequent Deployments. There is a need to Create the building blocks of digital transformation such as technology modernization, user experience design, DevOps, quality engineering, and agile. Automating quality engineering is needed to support a robust DevOps process. The ability to certify the product release without any manual effort enables quicker release cycles during the product development journey.

Organizations tend to lose focus post investment in Test Automation leading to a lack of monitoring around Maturity and Return on Investment (ROI) for Automation refinement. Tracking ROI and Maturity of Test Automation is no longer a "nice to have" but a necessity in Agile Organizations.

Proposed Solution: Rhino is a pluggable dashboard which can be integrated with most common test frameworks that aggregate the execution results, runs analytics, and scores the effectiveness and maturity of your automation framework. Rhino also provides easy filtering to remove noise, AI capabilities to tag test cases automatically, and offers insights into common trends and patterns of possible scenarios that might fail within the code that will add value to the engineering team. The Vision is to get into the Practitioner's approach of Prescriptive Analytics to bridge the last-mile gap between Test Automation and DevOps.

<u>Technologies Used:</u> Python, GraphQL, PostgreSQL, HTML5, CSS, and React.js

2. Blockchain in Supply Chain Management

<u>Idea USP:</u> Creating a single source of the truth to provide the business with transparency and provenance, reduce cost and complexity, geolocalize merchandise, reduce fraud, and enable a personalized interactive dashboard. This increases stakeholder/participant trust and overall satisfaction by powering a better and more relevant experience.

<u>Business Challenge:</u> Supply Chain Management ecosystems are facing problems due to a lack of information transparency and trust. Traditional supply chains contain a combination of paper-based processes and digital systems, where information is held up in 'silos.' Lack of end-to-end insight and process integration of information sharing results in gaps in tracking and tracing of products. These are key elements of digital supply chains. Changing consumer behavior and market conditions demand higher supply chain visibility and responsiveness. Traditional methods are, however, slow, fragmented, and ineffective. This makes it problematic to validate a products origin, location, or specific characteristics.

<u>Proposed Solution:</u> This Minimally Viable Product (MVP) is an application in the Fast Moving Consumer Goods (FMCG) foods supply chain based on the blockchain. A future enhancement is to add Electronic Product Code (EPC) Information Services that will help in inventory management. The management architecture for the company of the on-chain and off-chain data part of this solution, which can handle the

prodigious amount of data generated in the traditional Supply Chain. An enterprise-level smart contract is designed to prevent data tampering and disclosure of sensitive information across interactions among participants.

Technologies Used: This MVP was implemented based on the Blockchain Platform Open Source Hyperledger Fabric Framework. We used Hyperledger-Composer components for development and to build the Business network.

Innovation and Experimentation—Keys to Business Success

Transformation by itself does not ensure business success. Companies need to reimagine their business models and embrace innovation and experimentation to achieve sustainable growth. Those organizations that are willing to take chances and accept risk put themselves in a better position to not only survive disruption, but thrive.

The key is to take a holistic approach to digital innovation, including products, processes, and experiences. It is important to remember that digital innovation is not a one-and-done proposition; it is a continuous process of looking for opportunities to transform how things are done.

The innovation framework should include digital culture, talent, a technology platform, and governance. By leveraging these components, companies can achieve outcomes such as faster time to market with enhanced customer experience, and more cost-effective business operations.

Chapter 5

SELF-SERVICE BUSINESS DIGITAL PLATFORM: A GAME CHANGER FOR DIGITAL BUSINESS

DIGITAL TECHNOLOGY IS DRIVING INNOVATION, ACCELER-ATING business productivity, opening new channels of growth, and delivering superlative customer experience in most forward-looking organizations globally. Technology is no longer just a support function.

However, transitioning from a conventional, non-technology business to a full-fledged digital technology-driven business is no cakewalk. This switch is often hampered by challenges in change management, technology complexities, a shortage of skilled technology resources, and a lack of true collaboration among teams. This is especially true of enterprises that are still transitioning from legacy systems and that have fierce competition from digital natives.

The graphic below shows some of the most pressing technology challenges faced by organizations globally, and their potential impact on business.

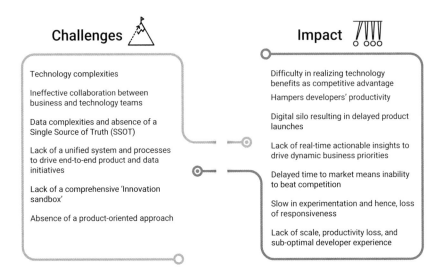

Considering the multiple challenges enterprises are facing in their digital journey, what is required today is a robust, open, integrated, self-service business digital platform that drives all the technology initiatives and lets business and technology teams collaborate effectively to build digital and data-centric products.

The following points underline the importance of deploying a self-service business digital platform to centralize business operations, data management, and workflow management; to deliver an SSOT; and to drive business insights.

Need for a Single Source of Truth

Modern business enterprises are witnessing a paradigm shift in digital business, delivering speed and enhanced customer experience. This shift is possible when the organization is empowered with an SSOT by integrating the complete digital ecosystem.

> "Modern business enterprises are witnessing a paradigm shift in digital business, delivering speed and enhanced customer experience. This shift is possible when the organization is empowered with a single source of truth by integrating the complete digital ecosystem."

Leveraging Data as Competitive Advantage

Roughly, a whopping 2.5 quintillion bytes of data is created every day. This data, generated by disparate sources, brings along challenges in terms of redundancy, accuracy, completeness, and consistency. It must be cleansed, processed, and transformed into business insights. Enterprises are increasingly investing in robust data platforms with out-of-the-box AI/ML capabilities to create data models.

Shift to the Cloud—and the Need for Security

Today, the cloud has been fully ingrained into the enterprise ecosystem. Hybrid cloud is gaining prominence, as enterprises seek out flexibility, scalability, business continuity, and control. As organizations balance the perfect mix of public and private clouds, they also need strong security protection and data access.

Faster Time to Market as Differentiator

Modern agile methods of application development have accelerated the development lifecycle and resulted in faster time to market for digital products. Continuous assessment and improvement of processes are required to adopt the modern ways of delivering business applications.

Need for Enhanced Productivity

In today's "techcelerated" business world, keeping pace with changing trends and technologies is essential. Enterprises want to remain focused on creating the most customer-centric products and business solutions. They have recognized the importance of the automated workflows and processes offered by self-service digital platforms. This automation is eliminating human errors in the development lifecycles, enhancing productivity by more than 30%, and accelerating the conception-to-commercialization journey.

Technology Rationalization

A mature self-service business digital platform helps enterprises simplify the process of standardizing useful technology stacks and eliminating redundant ones across processes and operations. Thanks to the automation delivered by the platform, enterprises need fewer tools to use, maintain, and manage, thus reducing the effort and total cost of ownership for portfolio management. Predefined process templates, configuration templates, and workflow templates in the platform make this process all the more easy for end users.

Modularization with Reusable Assets and Capabilities

To keep up with rapidly changing market dynamics, enterprises need modularization with open architecture. Modern digital platforms are adopting the modularization approach. Digital products developed on such platforms can more easily be modified, recompiled, updated, and upgraded than with traditional monolithic architectures. These platforms also promote the reuse of many components in the codebase and thus, enable enterprises to quickly develop products that scale.

Collaboration Among Business and Technology Teams

Breaking down silos is necessary. Teams across the enterprise must be aligned toward the single common business objective: Customer satisfaction. And to achieve this, a single platform is required for all—executives, business teams, engineering teams, analysts, and others.

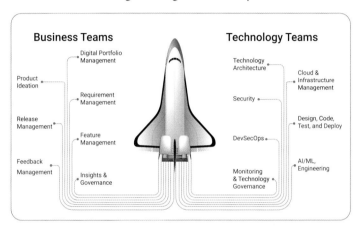

An end-to-end, integrated, self-service business digital platform can become a game changer in the growth journey of an enterprise. By focusing on simplification and collaboration, companies can deconstruct the legacy roadblocks that prevent agility and speed. In the new digital landscape, a self-service platform becomes the nexus driving collaboration and orchestration across all the partnered systems and stakeholders.

Using a self-service business digital platform can deliver several key business and technology benefits, as illustrated in the graphics below.

> "An end-to-end, integrated, self-service business digital platform can become a game changer in the growth journey of an enterprise."

Business Benefits

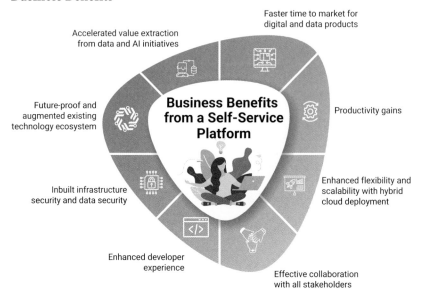

Accelerated value extraction from data and AI initiatives

Faster time to market for digital and data products

Future-proof and augmented existing technology ecosystem

Productivity gains

Inbuilt infrastructure security and data security

Enhanced flexibility and scalability with hybrid cloud deployment

Enhanced developer experience

Effective collaboration with all stakeholders

Technology Benefits

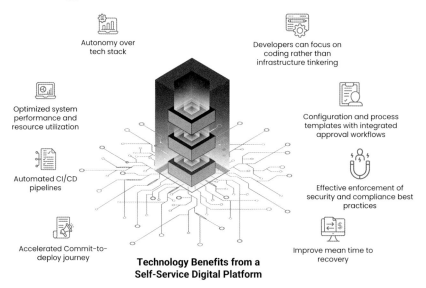

Autonomy over tech stack

Developers can focus on coding rather than infrastructure tinkering

Optimized system performance and resource utilization

Configuration and process templates with integrated approval workflows

Automated CI/CD pipelines

Effective enforcement of security and compliance best practices

Accelerated Commit-to-deploy journey

Improve mean time to recovery

Technology Benefits from a Self-Service Digital Platform

How can organizations ensure they are choosing the right self-service business digital platform approach? The following table lists three options for switching from a conventional operational approach to a self-service business digital platform, along with their pros and cons.

Scenario Number	Option	Pros	Cons
1	Building the self-service platform in-house	• Customized platform per specific needs	• Resource-intensive and complex to build • Steep learning curve and many times lack futuristic vision
2	Subscribing to specialized self-service platforms for each capability	• Specialized abilities for specific needs • Option to pick best-in-class product for each capability	• Integration of multiple products • Heavy investment • Lack of collaboration • Too many tools and vendors to manage
3	Subscribing to one end-to-end self-service digital platform that takes care of all capabilities.	• One comprehensive platform to drive all digital business initiatives • True collaboration between teams • Teams can focus on innovation without worrying about technology complexities	There are few platforms that might not be modular in design

Each organization must choose the best option depending on its internal skill set, budgets, and overall business and digital strategy. However, option three, subscribing to an end-to-end platform that is fully integrated, modular, scalable, and secure, has clear benefits that the others lack.

Such a platform must be instrumental in end-to-end business portfolio management, product development life-cycle management, data management and security, and DevOps management. Following are the key capabilities that make a self-service business digital platform ideal. Such a platform is bound to accelerate the idea-to-production journey for an enterprise and ensure superlative business outcomes.

Digital Portfolio Management	End-to-End PDLC Management	Data Platform with AI/ML out of the Box	Integrated DevSecOps
• Portfolio prioritization • Measurable product and process maturity • Financial performance	• Idea to Product • Design capabilities • Integrated tech stack and toolchain • Executive dashboards	• Data ingestion to insigths journey • AI/ML out-of-the-box • Data security and compliance	• Faster product development to deployment • Continuous risk assessment and monitoring

It must be one platform for all stakeholders, managing different responsibilities at various levels of the digital innovation and transformation agenda. This ranges from executives to portfolio managers; from product managers to program managers; from release managers to process owners, DevOps managers, data engineers and data scientists, developers and quality assurance specialists.

The platform can and should be valuable for everyone creating value for customers.

When such a readily developed platform is available as a service in the market, it does not make sense to spend resources on developing a platform internally.

Ideation to Deployment

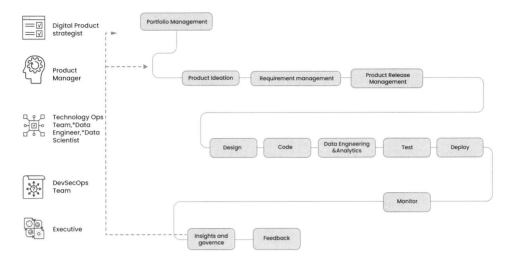

Getting Started

So far, we've discussed the challenges faced by organizations aspiring to become digital natives and that need a self-service business digital platform as a competitive advantage. We considered various options to choose the right platform and explained why subscribing to an end-to-end fully integrated scalable platform is important.

Many enterprises fail to understand the complexities involved in the ideation-to-productization process. Especially in the case of large teams distributed across geographies and working on complex enterprise solutions, the management and operationalization of so many technology stacks, tool chains, and license management efforts can be resource-intensive. Subscribing to an efficient self-service business digital platform is half the battle won.

However, the transition from legacy systems to adopting a self-service business digital platform takes effort and commitment from the organization and the cross-functional teams. The proper transition activities are crucial, as they lead to the actual realization of benefits.

Here is a recommended set of activities that can help you get started with a self-service portal. The good news is that each of these activities can be fast tracked and simplified by leveraging the platform. Otherwise, they could take weeks or even months, resulting in loss of productivity. These activities can be classified under three categories:

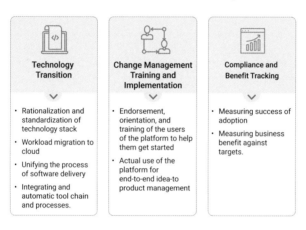

Here is a brief representation of all technology transition activities, which make up a majority of the effort.

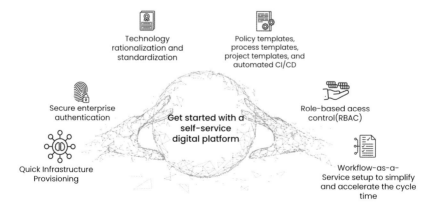

The self-service digital platform simplifies the overall complexities and makes the transition seamless and faster.

Accelerating Application Development

Let us consider an example of developing a web application leveraging a self-service portal to accelerate the overall idea-to-product journey. A typical project template in the platform standardizes the following aspects:

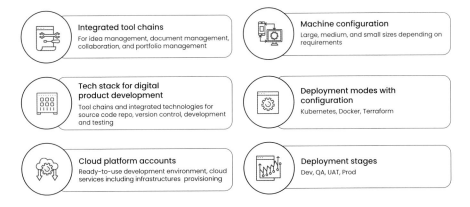

The use of the policy templates, process templates, configuration templates, and automated workflows for approvals eliminates the dependency and waiting period, accelerating the idea-to-market journey.

Accelerating Data Analytics Application Development

A self-service portal with data intelligence capabilities provides the following for creating a data engineering or data science application:

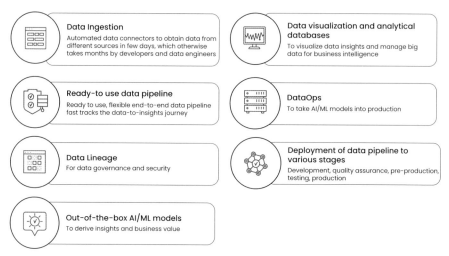

Data Ingestion
Automated data connectors to obtain data from different sources in few days, which otherwise takes months by developers and data engineers

Data visualization and analytical databases
To visualize data insights and manage big data for business intelligence

Ready-to use data pipeline
Ready to use, flexible end-to-end data pipeline fast tracks the data-to-insights journey

DataOps
To take AI/ML models into production

Data Lineage
For data governance and security

Deployment of data pipeline to various stages
Development, quality assurance, pre-production, testing, production

Out-of-the-box AI/ML models
To derive insights and business value

Here are some real-world examples of how businesses across the globe are embracing digital platforms for optimal utilization of available resources, enhanced productivity, and accelerated idea-to-product journey.

Novartis Improves Release Management, Rationalizes Technology Stack, and Automates Maturity Assessment

The digital research and development team of Novartis, a globally renowned pharmaceutical giant, had a huge repository of data sets related to biomedical research, drug development, and clinical research. Based on this data, Novartis wanted to plan and deliver predictable, coordinated, and well-orchestrated releases of the work to its customers.

However, due to limited automation, the team was experiencing productivity loss and complexities in project execution, release management, and product maturity assessment processes. This also led to suboptimal visibility and communication across the technology planning and customer success teams.

Novartis was trying to address the following challenges in its product and portfolio management:

Manual processes

The team still relied on several manual processes. As a result, the execution was time-consuming, tedious, and error-prone leading to productivity loss.

Limited automation of maturity assessment

The maturity of the products and processes were assessed by responses solicited from the users and were difficult to verify in the absence of system-supported data.

Lack of centralized and integrated system

Processes were driven by conventions. Data and information were scattered across disjointed repositories. This limited the ability to scale up and seamless execution.

Absence of seamless tracking, visibility, and communication

In absence of unified systems, it was difficult and complex to manage and communicate across distributed products and teams.

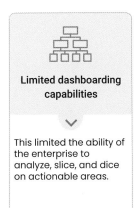

Limited dashboarding capabilities

This limited the ability of the enterprise to analyze, slice, and dice on actionable areas.

To overcome these challenges, Novartis embraced an end-to-end self-service business digital platform.

By leveraging the end-to-end management capabilities of the platform, Novartis could:

- Achieve overall productivity gains.

- Drive faster release cycles and improve overall product release orchestration and execution efficiency.
- Unite business, product, and technology teams to effectively manage product and portfolios in line with customer requirements, leading to increased customer satisfaction.
- Automate maturity assessment across processes, teams, and technology capabilities in real time.
- Leverage reusable components in the platform, leading to faster time to market at more competitive costs.
- Use insightful executive dashboards to make real-time decisions.

All in all, the adoption of a self-service business digital platform certainly steered Novartis toward quicker, smarter, and data-driven business outcomes.

NatureSweet Makes the Most of Data Intelligence and Web Application Capabilities to Improve Revenue Prediction

NatureSweet Ltd., a leading grower, packager, and seller of produce, wanted to improve yield prediction accuracy, customer fill-rate, and revenues from top accounts. The traditional data collection and forecasting methods the company used were highly resource-intensive and time consuming. This often led to a lack of accuracy. NatureSweet wanted to leverage data science, forecasting techniques and automated data pipeline for yield prediction. Furthermore, the company wanted to develop a planning simulator to accurately model the possible planting cycles to meet market demand and make necessary adjustments based on several factors. This is a strategic platform for planning to reduce manual work, improve operational efficiency and flexibility to use machine learning algorithms in the future.

NatureSweet encountered few challenges due to disparate sources of data, absence of single source of truth, quality of historical data, complexities in managing data pipeline and limited data science or machine learning in yield forecasting methods to improve yield forecasting.

The company adopted a self-service digital platform and empowered its business and IT team including vendor partners to build an automated data analytics and business applications solution. By making the most of the data intelligence and business application development capabilities of the platform, NatureSweet could overcome its business challenges in the following ways:

- Seamlessly ingest farming data in an automated data pipeline developed and customized in the self-service business digital platform. This data was collected from disparate sources such as mobile-agri apps, sensors, drones, farming machinery, robotic devices, and IoT devices, and in various formats such as Excel workbooks, Microsoft Word files, PDFs, and CSV files, among others.
- By leveraging the data visualization features of the platform, the enterprise could: achieve better sales forecasting, gain insights about geographical market share, streamline agri-food supply chain, and enhance the customer experience.
- When this data gets processed by using the robust customizable AI/ML models in the platform, the accuracy of yield prediction is expected to increase by up to 30%.
- For the new planning simulator application performance and run times will be significantly optimized from the current levels to improve user experience

Due to the data-driven business decisions, the company can meet the demand to focus on achieving higher revenue with all the benefits of smart farming, thus making it a win-win situation for NatureSweet and its consumers.

SaaS Company Builds a Stronger Product Pipeline and Delivery Capability to Drive Customer Acquisition

A fast-growing software-as-a-service (SaaS) company that creates simplified technology for small businesses has created a platform that empowers these businesses by providing everything they need in one place to stay connected with their new and repeat customers.

The company's cloud-based suite of mobile and web tools transform the way small businesses run their operations. It is in the process of revamping its business model to drive an exponential increase in the number of customers as well as provide more value to customers, and is taking a multi-pronged approach to achieve this.

There are parallel business initiatives, including growth, to drive the acquisition of new customers and retain existing customers with greater business value and better core products; fintech, to provide better payments, subscription experience and to connect small and mid-sized enterprises (SMEs) to lending companies; and a platform to integrate with other SME products and allow partner companies to integrate with the company's products.

The business hired a digital partner to implement its business strategy and get its products ready for exponential growth. A bootstrap team was put together consisting of product and technology leaders from both organizations. After multiple discussions and brainstorming sessions, the bootstrap team came up with a set of recommendations and architecture proposal based on their assessment.

The proposed architecture was a revamp of the existing monolithic system into a microservices-based cloud native application. Multiple cross-functional teams, aligned to specific business goals, were set up to put the strategy into action.

Each team is focusing on specific projects under the business initiatives (growth, fintech, and platform.) The objective is to move the needle on specific business KPIs by developing new services and enhancing user experience. Teams are adopting a fail-fast approach by iteratively releasing the features to customers and learning from customer feedback.

Different teams have worked on parallel projects under the business initiatives. The project that is part of the growth initiative was to revamp the company's marketing site to provide an experience that clearly depicts the value proposition of the company's products. This is achieved by providing an interactive experience to help evaluate various products without having to create an account.

The fintech project focused on integrating with a new payment partner that provides a smooth merchant onboarding experience and an intuitive payment experience. This integration was done both on the web and via mobile apps to provide a seamless experience across the devices.

One of the platform projects was to provide a better first-time experience to merchants by automatically synchronizing the data from its other accounts, such as Google My Business, Facebook, and QuickBooks. A new authentication service based on AWS Cognito was developed. Also, the company's product was integrated with Google, Facebook, and QuickBooks APIs to fetch and upload the data from and to those accounts.

In addition, two proof-of-concept platforms were developed: a developer portal and an app store. The developer portal provides information to partners and third-party developers about the various APIs exposed by the company and allows them to sign up for a developer account. They can use these APIs to develop applications that would integrate their products with the SaaS company's products.

App Store, on the other hand, showcases the apps complementing the company's offering, including apps that can help SMEs grow their business and save time. Both these platforms will be iterated over to build a large ecosystem of partners and developers.

The business impact of the projects will be measured continuously and used to learn and improve systems.

Thriving in the Digital Era

If organizations take the right approach, a self-service business digital platform can indeed be a game changer for digital business. As we've seen, shifting from legacy systems to a modern technology infrastructure that supports digital business is not an easy task. The transformation involves challenges in change management, technology complexities, the shortage of skilled professionals, and others.

Despite these hurdles, companies need to move ahead into the digital era. The simple fact is that they have no choice. To compete in today's environment businesses cannot cling to the old ways of doing things. A robust self-service business digital platform drives technology initiatives and enables business and technology leaders and teams to collaborate effectively to build digital and data-centric products.

By focusing on this collaboration as well as simplification, companies can knock down any legacy roadblocks preventing them from being agile and fast to market. In the emerging digital landscape, a self-service business digital platform is the solution that makes true transformation possible, and allows businesses to thrive in this new environment.

Chapter 6

OPERATIONALIZING DIGITAL BUSINESS ACROSS THE ENTERPRISE

Most CEOs today know the companies they lead need to become digital businesses to remain relevant in their markets. But for many, frustration is growing as companies struggle to transition from traditional business models.

Research firm Gartner has noted that organizations are accelerating digital transformation processes for long-term growth and profitability. Yet many of the organizations the firm has researched "remain untested in the face of digital challenge and their digital transformation readiness is therefore uncertain," it said.

Many enterprises launch digital transformation programs, led by technology, which are slow, expensive, and fail to deliver business value. Other companies are creating new organizations focused on digital, but soon become siloed and distanced from actual business opportunities and challenges that require innovation and quick action.

With technology being fully integrated in business models that are changing at lightning speed today, CEOs and other enterprise leaders must address the digital challenge for long-term and material business performance improvements.

While many enterprises are in the midst of digital transformations with differing scopes and mixed results, to truly operationalize digital business leaders must address four areas: people/process, data, technology, and sponsorship.

> "With technology being fully integrated in business models that are changing at lightning speed today, CEOs and other enterprise leaders must address the digital challenge for long-term and material business performance improvements."

People/Process

Most enterprises have a talented employee base, with many years of company and industry knowledge. These individuals know how business has been performed and what has been successful in the past. But that does not necessarily translate into future success. These experiences and knowledge of how the company operates is especially important. But it can also be a hinderance in today's fast-changing world.

In the digital environment, workforces that are willing to leverage industry expertise and to take chances on new business models supported by data and technology have the best chance to pivot to a digital business. In other words: think big, fail fast, learn, repeat.

For companies to do this successfully, leaders must focus on a small part of the workforce, typically 5% to 10% of the organization. The reason why it is so small is due to the nature of how work is being done.

Typically, 90% of the organization is managing current business, with the remaining focused on new capabilities.

Leaders must ensure that this small cohort focused on digital and new business models has the right mindset and skills. Individuals and teams in this digital space must be willing to take chances and fail.

Normally, innovation is difficult when people are focused on business-critical operations and processes. If something fails, the company is drastically impacted. But at the same time, teams cannot be housed in an ivory tower, far away from the day-to-day operations or market pressures.

Teams must have the right mix of current business operations knowhow and the right data and technology skills to understand the art of possibility. They also need time, tools, and funding to try new innovations and rapid prototyping. The digital teams must also have the right leadership and communication skills to convince the organization top to bottom of changes that need to be made for the good of the enterprise.

> "Teams must have the right mix of current business operations knowhow and the right data and technology skills to understand the art of possibility."

No longer can business throw needs over the fence to IT organizations, waiting months and sometimes years for IT to develop a solution and completely missing the mark because the business needs and direction have already changed.

In today's fast-changing markets, business and technology talents must be combined in product teams focused on delivering business outcomes and enterprise impact. These digital product teams normally have between 8 and 10 members, with several different skills sets.

The skill sets depend on the area of focus and the type of innovation or solution being developed. But in the majority of cases, teams will need business acumen and software development skills. They also need to start working in an agile approach, looking to deliver incremental value in two- to three-week sprints and working from a priority backlog.

While having internal skills is a must, it is very difficult in today's market to hire and retain top digital, data, and technology talent. Most organizations leverage a mix of internal and external talent. But it is important for companies to select external partners that come with the inherent digital culture that they aspire to themselves.

While the traditional, large technology services struggle, smaller and nimbler digitally native organizations can be a catalyst for providing world class digital and data resources, helping organizations develop a new culture that is fast moving, and focused on achieving business outcomes.

Data

For many organizations, until recently data has been an afterthought. As companies have grown, they have created data silos, storing information in disparate legacy systems that are leveraging hundreds of technologies.

Within these systems, much of the data is of low quality, because of a minimum focus on quality that allows business transactions to take place properly. In addition, in many organizations data means power, and this is where the business data silos begin.

Due to culture or incentive issues, many departments within businesses do not share data with other parts of the organization, or even within the same business unit. Without this ability to bring data together, companies cannot tap into this veritable data gold mine waiting to be mined.

In order to create an SSOT, organizations need to understand where the data resides. Creating a data catalog that shows where data sits and what it represents is a must. To do this at an enterprise scale, there must be data owners who represent and curate enterprise data.

Data must be maintained at a functional level within research and development, commercial, and manufacturing areas. With this capability, data can be pulled together quickly to drive insights on internal data. And over time, creating SSOTs for business-related outcomes can evolve into an enterprise data environment that is the reference of all data inquiries and analysis.

Finally, the explosion of external data combining with this internal data has the potential to allow business and market insights that present unlimited value and opportunity.

Technology

While technologies such as ERP and CRM systems are important to enable day-to-day transactions, the newest digital and data technologies are fundamental for transforming enterprises into digital businesses.

As highlighted in the previous chapter, a self-service business digital platform is key to enabling digital business. With the fragmentation in the digital and data space, organizations are actually becoming slower, not faster. This runs counter to what a digital business needs to be—faster and more nimble than transitional businesses.

In addition to a self-service business digital platform that orchestrates and automates the digital and data ecosystem, businesses need to possess other fundamental capabilities.

One is the ability to migrate to the cloud. The trend is toward companies evolving toward a multi-cloud strategy, leveraging cloud services such as those offered by market leaders AWS, Microsoft Azure, and Google Cloud.

These providers drive innovation with different capabilities, and organizations need to tap into these. In addition, typically there are several other database and development solutions and tools that are required to develop digital solutions.

Having these capabilities and making continued investments in the latest technologies are a must, as new features in areas such as artificial intelligence and machine learning are evolving quickly.

Sponsorship

At most organizations, doing things in a different way is met with heavy resistance. When the same business models have been in place for a long time, changing the paradigm is difficult.

The last ingredient to fully operationalize digital business at enterprise level is sponsorship. Direct CEO/senior executive engagement, with a clear mandate to become a digital business, is fundamental.

This engagement includes continuous and consistent messaging that the organization needs to leverage technology and data in order to compete effectively. Also, it is imperative to have a consolidated business strategy that embeds digital capabilities. This enables new business models, automation, and data insights that will drive the business forward.

Ultimately, companies must dramatically increase speed to scale, operationalize, and iterate innovative digital solutions in order to compete with the digital-native companies in their space. Think of how quickly businesses such as Uber, Spotify, and Airbnb have grown in their markets.

Companies need to establish the right environment for their organization, including the very best people/processes, data, technology, and sponsorship, to stand a chance in this new digital world.

The following are examples of companies that are succeeding in their shift to digital business.

Garment Maker Uses Algorithm-Based Approach to Create Correlation Across Data Points and Extract Business Insights

One of the world's leading garment manufacturers has the unique distinction of managing the end-to-end cycle of ideation, product development, manufacturing, supply chain, and sales under one roof.

Traditionally, the company made garments based on its expertise and experience. With the emergence of mobile apps and social interactions, the company realized that it needed to align its business with the desires of customers.

The idea was to drive product development as part of a co-creation exercise along with its customers. The company decided to add more feedback mechanisms for customers visiting the store, which would provide a simple and effective way to co-create.

The company put in place a mechanism to collect various data points and store them in a single database. It analyzed data points from sales, marketing, e-commerce, store feedback, fashion trends and brought these into an SSOT.

The company used an algorithm-based approach to create correlation and causation across these data points, to extract insights from the unstructured data, and convert them into product ideas.

Walmart Focuses on Higher Digitalization in Nearly All Areas of its Business

Walmart spends more than $12 billion on technology, making it the third largest IT spender in the world behind Amazon and Alphabet. The retailer is going through a digital transformation and has shifted its focus from re-platforming its e-commerce business to re-platforming across the board.

The company created its digital arm, Walmart labs, to drive digital business not just in e-commerce but for a complete digital transformation across all divisions, to help business growth.

Walmart's traditional operating model was insufficient to serve customers' evolving needs in the U.S., and the rise of social media and millennials' consumption habits all required the businesses that wanted to serve them to adopt a better model driven by technology.

Walmart has focused on higher digitalization in nearly all areas of its business. From the supply chain to sales, customer service, marketing, and store operations, etc. Some examples are:

- Store management. Walmart's new Intelligent Retail Lab (IRL) focuses on driving the future of retail through innovations in stores via an impressive array of sensors, cameras, and processors.
- Inventory availability. Automating the inventory scanning process on shelves so that when customers come into a store, they will always get what they were looking for.

- Supply chain improvement. Walmart is using technologies such as AI and blockchain to track inventory down its supply chain.
- Price adjustments. Walmart is testing electric shelf labels in two stores in the U.S. to make price adjustments automatically as dictated by store management.
- Transportation. Walmart has implemented a data science methodology in the transportation process to optimize lane planning and route optimization in its transport management systems.
- Food traceability. Walmart is implementing a food safety blockchain solution to track food safety regulations and force suppliers to track their produce using blockchain technology as well.
- Customer analytics. Extensive use of big data to personalize its interaction with customers, drawing insights from data analyses on purchasing behavior, search histories, and web interactions. Its Data Cafe acquisition allows Walmart to model, manipulate, and visualize recent transactional data, and collect from more than 200 internal and external streams.
- Customer service. Walmart leverages machine learning, AI , and data platform solutions for a wide range of external customer-facing services and internal business applications.

New Novartis Application Brings Added Value from Data Science Team

Novartis' finance team wanted to enhance and re-engineer its existing predictive finance capabilities to overcome a slew of operational, architectural, and technology-stack difficulties that come with the current legacy platform.

The company set out to design and build an entirely cloud-based architecture using powerful tools such as AWS-Sagemaker, Snowflake, and Python AI/ML libraries, guided by the data platform architectural principles, including information security, to ensure scalability and high availability as well as deliver high performance. Another key requirement was to industrialize the AI/ML models at scale. Traceability and model tracking were also key considerations.

The new application and platform are designed to be extremely adaptable and maintainable, with high-quality software standards incorporated. It is also modular, well-documented, and certified.

Another key part of application design and implementation is ease of operations, including continuous integration/continuous delivery pipelines that enable continuous integration and delivery in the AI/ML platform. The system is metadata driven and configurable for increased flexibility, unlike the existing system, which lacks consistency and transparency

It was also designed to have a clear separation of data engineering pieces and core data science components. It also renders the highest level of parallelization at both the system level and application level and incorporates sophisticated resource monitoring mechanisms with the ability to recover from an interrupted/broken run, with ease.

This has now resulted in a new application that is predicated on a highly scalable infrastructure, flexible architecture (cloud agnostic), completely metadata-driven design with maximum parallel efficiency, and easy-to-maintain application with sophisticated ML-Ops pipeline integration.

The impact is that there is now clear separation of data engineering pieces and core data science components for a highly cohesive and de-coupled architecture, rendering operational ease so that the entire data science team can focus on delivering value-adds rather than expending their efforts on operations, tracking and maintenance. The new system also speeds up the learning curve for new data scientists, via well-organized, consistently written and modularized code.

With a combination of system- and application-level parallelization and sophisticated resource monitoring mechanisms, resources will be optimally utilized. This means that the company will see reduced manual intervention to run and maintain the ML models, better predictive analytics, and significant cost savings.

Altimetrik Digitizes Key Scenarios
and Associated Workflows for Business Operations

As we address the four key areas for operationalizing digital business, our next step is to digitize the key scenarios and their associated workflows for business operations. Business operations is all about data and the right visualization providing the right insights.

Traditionally, monitoring and dashboarding has been the way we used to think about digitizing business operations. But the future will be about presenting the data in the right way to predict and even suggest options using self-learning algorithms.

Business operations also involve a lot of compliance-related activities that fall under the purview of regulatory risk that needs to be taken care of as well. Timesheet entry is a good example of that. And the question that we should ask is, "How easy and seamless is that for all the parties involved?"

Digitization is always different from digitalization. Yes, many have actually digitized timesheets today. But have they been digitalized? This is just one example, and there are many others. Most of us are introduced to a lot of digitization, but how many of us are thinking about digitalization?

Digitalization is the key when it comes to making business operations a more productive and rewarding discipline that just elevates itself from being a reporting and discipline adherence team to an insight-driven value-adding team. Up to 80% of all business operations activities are actually employee engagement related.

Business operations is all about ensuring that all the functions of an organization work seamlessly and are able to work as if there are no boundaries across different teams.

At Altimetrik, we are creating an employee engagement platform that enables this. This platform will aggregate all the data involved during multiple employee journeys and provides a real-time, unified way for employees to engage and complete their key activities at the right time.

The platform will enable our employees to be more effective and productive and keep the organization informed about progress on various engagement avenues that we provide today. This is a data-driven approach toward business operations that will help provide the right insights to leadership.

The beauty of "data" is actually two things. One is the source of the data, and the other is the data itself. With our approach, we have been able to solve both. One, the data is sourced from the employees themselves, and two is we have templatized the data collection in such a way that it is cleaner and more normalized and will provide the insights we need.

We have a digitalized way of engaging with employees on day-to-day activities, and the information needed to understand the key performance indicators we want to see on our business operations dashboards.

Adopting this kind of process will help companies move forward in a powerful way in this data-driven era.

Bringing Digital to Life

Many companies are struggling to transition from traditional business models to digital business. They launch transformation programs that are slow and costly, and fail to deliver value to the organization or its customers.

Some organizations are hampered by siloed data, or there is disconnect between technology deployments and actual business needs. Regardless of the situation, the efforts involved in becoming a digital business can be wasted if solutions are not correctly put into practice.

In order to truly operationalize digital business, leaders including CEOs need to address the key areas of people/process, data, technology and sponsorship. By doing this, they can help ensure that their organizations are operationalizing digital business across the enterprise.

Chapter 7

BECOMING A DIGITAL BUSINESS—THE PATHWAY FORWARD

Transforming into a truly digital business means changing the way many day-to-day processes and operations are conducted within your organization. It can be a difficult journey that requires hard work and is not without risk. But it is necessary in order to remain competitive and thrive in today's business world.

Indeed, there is a sense of inevitability about being digital. As consulting firm Deloitte has noted, "before long, every business will be a digital business. CEOs must make explicit choices about their strategy to win in a digital economy."

The journey involves a number of key components; embracing simplification and an agile culture; creating a single source of truth; fostering innovation and experimentation; implementing a digital platform; and operationalizing digital business across the enterprise.

The current environment of frequent mergers, acquisitions, and joint ventures has created silos and complex business operations. This is further complicated by fragmented ERP and IT systems that create complexity, and companies are not able to effect change through simplification.

Any change becomes complex and takes enterprises a long time to complete, making it difficult to get the insights and visibility they need into their end-to-end value chain. If companies cannot make the transition to digital business, they will find it difficult to compete effectively and grow.

Digital business addresses the challenges of this environment by centralizing business operations and creating a self-service business digital platform that leverages current digital technology. When companies make the transition to operate as a digital business, they develop agility, build effective collaboration across the organization, and create end-to-end insights needed to make better decisions at speed.

> "When companies make the transition to operate as a digital business, they develop agility, build effective collaboration across the organization, and create end-to-end insights needed to make better decisions at speed."

This simplifies the process for the business to bring data together from across the organization, from transactional systems and platforms such as ERP and CRM. It does not touch business operations, only the data.

Digital business by itself can help enterprise growth—revenue, profit, market share—with speed, through an incremental approach.

Many companies are in the midst of digital transformations involving technology and the business. Some are farther along than others. Irrespective of where they are in their digital maturity, they can move forward with the following pathway to become digital businesses.

An Incremental Approach

Digital business on its own takes an incremental approach focused on prioritized outcomes leveraging a self-service business digital platform for all operations.

A differentiator of digital business is that it produces effective outcomes quickly. Because of the speed and agility associated with a digital business, it is not dependent on the digital transformation of any specific business. Companies can start to become a digital business focused on business outcomes immediately. Here are some key steps:

- The CEO and executive team set the priorities on outcomes. Many of these can be accomplished simultaneously with business leadership and engineering teams, through an agile approach over the following two years.
- The CEO and executive team need to set the culture of digital business, taking ownership of each outcome. The culture includes simplification of end-to-end workflows and collaboration in an agile way. The teams converge on an SSOT for intelligent decision-making and effective outcomes. Through the use of AI and ML, real-time data, and an SSOT, the organization can make better predictions.
- The CEO and executive team Identify dedicated internal teams from the business and technology areas who can take ownership and collaborate within an agile culture.
- Companies need to identify a strategic partner that can help them build solutions for specific outcomes. They can work together to achieve the simplification of end-to-end workflows, and create an agile approach to collaboration. Many companies do not have the experience or expertise to accomplish this on their own. A stra-

tegic partner can also innovate over a self-service business digital platform that can bring data from various sources, through an end-to-end orchestration of solutions, with a higher degree of productivity. And a strategic partner can also help to internalize the digital culture for customer teams that create scale. Over time, the partner can continue to supplement and complement these teams.

- The CEO and executive team need to monitor outcomes on a regular basis. They also should continue to ensure a culture of collaboration, agility, continuous innovation, and experimentation that drives growth.

Digital Transformation Through a Business Lens

A self-service digital ecosystem is created by rationalizing and leveraging the current technology landscape and new digital technologies. This will save a substantial amount of investment for the enterprise across license fees and building the skills required to support that.

This also enables a culture of increased speed, discipline and consistency, and the higher productivity needed to become a digital business at scale. This can be achieved in a short timeframe on an incremental basis. Digital transformation focused on business outcomes can start immediately.

The path to digital technology transformation to create growth requires using a business lens coupled with taking an incremental approach to eliminate silos and centralizing all operations in this self-service business digital platform, rather than relying on transactional systems such as ERP.

For many organizations that have been doing things the same way for many years, it is very difficult in terms of both building an agile culture and eliminating siloes. It is crucial for the CEO and executive team, including digital technology leaders, to set an incremental approach with a business lens to establish priorities.

This will provide the support to the business that will bring and end-to-end environment with security, compliance, quality, and reliability. Additionally, executive teams set the discipline so that technology teams adhere to an agile culture and end-to-end collaboration with the business.

This will result in higher productivity and will also enhance the technology asset rationalization in terms of effectiveness and simplification of skills required. In essence, it will reduce the current technology investments substantially.

A digital partner can create the end-to-end environment for collaboration with an incremental approach, and leverage existing technology assets by rationalizing them. Some enterprises have already invested in a business digital platform. A digital partner can also be the catalyst to help rationalize the technology and create an end-to-end orchestration in a disciplined way.

Across the enterprise there will be greater consistency among the engineering teams in how they collaborate with the business, bring high productivity, and generate effective outcomes. This will help create scale across the enterprise and eliminate the silos that hamper growth. The technology environment brings end-to-end security and creates reusable assets for productivity, high quality, reliability, and compliance.

> "Digital transformation with a business lens drives outcomes effectively with speed."

The combination of digital business on its own and alignment to digital transformation with a business lens will help companies achieve business outcomes effectively with speed and scale. It will help enterprises achieve business outcomes and reduce overall technology investments as well as the cost of managing them. The combination of technology and workflow tool rationalization will lead to substantial savings in license fees as well as the skills required to support these activities.

A critical component is talent and a culture of agility, collaboration, innovation, and simplification. That is the reason the executive team including the CEO needs to establish and enforce this type of culture and make it a priority to find the appropriate talent.

Many enterprises are slowly moving to this approach, both large and midsize. One of the top financial services technology companies adopted this through a digital partner, and started seeing outcomes without disrupting the current business. It also focused on modernizing its platform in the cloud. Now that the same digital partner is helping the company internalize this to create scale across the organization.

"A critical component is talent and a culture of agility, collaboration, innovation, and simplification. That is the reason the executive team including the CEO needs to establish and enforce this type of culture and make it a priority to find the appropriate talent."

Similarly, the CEO of a major pharmaceutical company set the direction for the culture, where business and technology are collaborating consistently across the enterprise. That includes creating an SSOT and reusable data and product assets.

The company needed help from a digital partner to create an agile culture with the help of technology practitioners, an end-to-end collaborative environment, and an SSOT for business outcomes. The partner also helped create an environment for innovation and experimentation. In a few years, the company will internalize this culture across the enterprise for scale on a continuous basis.

Another example comes from the auto manufacturing sector. After a series of mergers and acquisitions, a global auto manufacturer/supplier was left with disjointed data systems, silos, and disparate product masters and charter accounts.

The company struggled to manage data across different ERPs, CRMs, and other systems centrally, and decided to undertake the creation of a central business group to build a standard product master and charter accounts across business functions mapped into each individual group for an SSOT.

The company's priority is to focus on business-led ownership to coordinate and build the business unit SSOTs. It decided to create account/product masters for sales, production, supply chain, etc., and enable finance to tap into them.

Information from various sources will be brought into a self-service business digital platform to leverage product and account masters, so the data could be consolidated into an enterprise SSOT. Each group's business team will have full ownership and work in collaboration with engineering teams in a true agile approach.

The goal is to create a culture of collaboration and iterative processes to converge data into an SSOT, and to make better decisions without disruption to the current business.

Enterprises are being presented with a golden opportunity to transform from their current complex business operations through the simplification of both business and technologies, with an agile culture that leverages a single source of truth and Innovation—to create unlimited opportunities for growth.

This is by no means an easy task. Due to the inherent challenges of such a transformation and the ongoing shortage of talent, companies need to bring in a team of experts that can be a catalyst and strategic partner, to help create the environment of simplification and collaboration.

Working together, they can ensure a successful transition from the old to the new, from the traditional business of the past to the digital business of the future.

Digital business is the catalyst for bringing organizations together to effect tangible and lasting change.

Much has been written about the digital transformation, including the downsides. In a recent post, Forbes estimated that a staggering 84% or so of digital transformation projects fail, and according to analysts at Ovum only 8% of executives think their organization's transformation was entirely successful.

In a digital transformation, the tasks and outcomes are largely owned by the CIO and IT organization. But in building a digital business, the value of the CIO's role is expanded through meaningful partnerships with colleagues in the C-suite, who define and own the desired business strategy and outcomes.

Mark Twain said "A person who won't read has no advantage over one who can't read." This holds equally true in failing to grasp the significance of building a digital business. The fundamental advantages one gains through simplification, speed, and efficiency are best realized by digital business practices.

Digital transformation is important, but takes a broad-scale approach with a longer timeframe to realize outcomes. Having the ability to leverage the current infrastructure and immediately gain insights from real-time data across the enterprise is what delivers a single source of truth—and near-term value.

Digital business is the pathway to exceed expectations of what can be achieved by reducing complexity, delivering transparency, increasing speed of execution, and accelerating growth.

GLOSSARY OF TERMS

Advanced analytics—Analysis of data using sophisticated tools and techniques, such as data/text mining, machine learning, forecasting, visualization, sentiment analysis, network and cluster analysis, simulation, complex event processing, and neural networks, to gain deeper business insights.

Agile software development—An iterative approach to software development that is designed to help teams deliver products to market more quickly. The Agile methodology breaks up projects into several phases and involves constant collaboration among team members and key stakeholders, as well as continuous improvement at every stage.

Application programming interface (API)—A software interface that provides a connection between software programs or computer systems. An API specification is a document or standard that describes how to build or use an API. The term API can refer to the specification or the implementation.

Artificial intelligence (AI)—Intelligence that is demonstrated by machines, as compared with natural intelligence displayed by humans. AI can include any system that perceives its environment and takes actions to maximize its chance of achieving its goals.

Business digital platform (BDP)—A platform that integrates into an enterprise's existing digital ecosystem and automates activities that would otherwise be done manually by software and data engineers. It provides transparency into process bottlenecks and technology issues, and ensures discipline by employing agile and development processes as well as the collaborative culture required for digital business success.

Business simplification—A way of thinking rather than a set of action items, business simplification involves continuously simplifying all aspects of the business, including processes, products, and data management. Shifting the mindset of an organization to embrace simplification takes practice and training, but simplification is vital for sustainable business growth.

Collation—One of the keys to a successful single source of truth strategy, collation is the process of bringing data from multiple systems such as enterprise resource planning (ERP), product lifecycle management (PLM), marketing, sales, finance, and management and storing them into a closely related structure.

Customer relationship management (CRM)—A process in which an organization administers all of its interactions with customers, typically using data analytics to study large volumes of data to draw insights. CRM platforms compile data from various communications channels such as websites, calls, emails, live chat, and social media.

Data federation—The ability, using a software platform, to aggregate data from disparate sources in a virtual database so it can be used for data analysis. The virtual database does not contain the data itself but rather information about the actual data and its location.

Data science—A field that uses scientific methods, processes, algorithms, and systems to extract insights from structured and unstructured data and apply those insights across a range of business applications. The concept of data science unifies data analysis, statistics, and related methods to better understand and analyze actual phenomena with data.

Data silos—An insular data management strategy in which one system or subsystem is not capable of interacting with others even though they might be related. Silos in some cases prevent information from being adequately shared among groups or departments, hindering opportunities to gain business insights.

Data simplification—An initiative that seeks to eliminate the rigidity and complexity of how data is created, stored, and used in an organization. A key to data simplification is taking an independent approach to developing a single source of truth to make faster, better decisions.

DevOps—A set of practices that combines software development and IT operations, DevOps is designed to shorten the software development lifecycle and provide continuous delivery of products and features of high quality. It complements the agile software development methodology.

DevSecOps—A proactive approach to software security that anticipates possible threats and vulnerabilities and remediates them before they become a problem. With DevSecOps, an extension of DevOps, teams review, audit, and test software code for security issues on a regular basis, and address issues as soon as they arise.

Digital business—An organization that leverages technology and data to focus on business outcomes for growth and continuous innovation. It involves taking an incremental approach to using existing resources to achieve bite-sized outcomes; using data intelligently to make smarter decisions; focusing on simplification and collaboration; and employing continuous innovation and experimentation at speed with low investment.

Digital culture—A corporate culture that emphasizes the importance of digital services, processes, and technologies. Among the key characteristics of digital culture are agility, data-driven design, innovation and risk taking, customer centricity, and strong collaboration.

Digital transformation—An organizational effort driven by technology and focused on significant transformation in terms of talent, culture, and processes. It takes a broad-scale, application-based approach that typically requires heavy investment and a lot of time to complete.

Enterprise resource planning (ERP)—The integrated management of key business processes such as finance/accounting, human resources, supply chain, and sales and marketing, often in real time. ERP functions are provided by software platforms, generally a suite of integrated applications, that operate on premises or in the cloud.

Innovation and experimentation—In the context of digital business, innovation and experimentation means creating next-generation digital strategies and newer business models and channels, and unlocking radical efficiency gains that are enabled by digital technologies. Digital businesses need to take a holistic approach to digital innovation and experimentation, including product innovation, process innovation, and experience innovation. In all three cases technology drives the innovation.

Machine learning (ML)—A component of artificial intelligence, machine learning is the study of computer algorithms that can improve automatically through experience and the use of data. Algorithms build a model based on sample data known as training data, so they can make predictions or decisions without being explicitly programmed to do so.

Metadata management—Involves managing metadata—data that provides information about other data but not the content of the data itself. It is the comprehensive process and governance framework for creating, controlling, enhancing, and managing a metadata schema, model, or other structured aggregation system.

Microservices—An architectural and organizational approach to software development, in which software is composed of small and independent services that communicate over application programming interfaces. With microservices architectures, applications can be easier to scale and faster to develop, speeding up time-to-market for new products and features.

Modularization—An approach for modern digital platforms that emphasizes reusable assets and capabilities, enabling to keep up with rapidly changing market dynamics. Digital products developed on such platforms can be easily modified, recompiled, updated, and upgraded than the traditional monolithic architecture.

Periodicity—Perhaps the most important aspect of single source of truth, periodicity covers factors such as how frequently data is being collated to understand the ongoing changes of the organization; how frequently insights are being generated from data and how frequently these insights and data are used by the organization.

Predictive analytics—A technique that leverages data mining, predictive modelling, and machine learning to analyze current and historical data in order to make predictions about future events. Predictive models use patterns in historical and transactional data to identify risks and opportunities.

Practitioners—Key members of a team who understand business and technology and are adept at breaking down challenges into smaller use cases to accelerate decision-making and quickly create new business models. Practitioners aim to deliver business outcomes through simplification of end-to-end workflows and collaboration between the business and technology.

Process simplification—An effort to reduce the complexity of business processes across the organization. This includes all functional units including operations, accounting and finance, human resources, IT, and others.

Product lifecycle management (PLM)—The process of managing the entire lifecycle of a product, including inception, design, manufacturing, testing, sales, maintenance, and retirement. The PLM software helps organizations create new products such as software and bring them to market efficiently.

Product simplification—An initiative that reduces the overall complexity of products and services by decreasing the complexity of making and managing a product or range of products.

Run ahead—The "run-ahead" team creates organizational changes within sprints, just as a development team creates product features within sprints. It focuses on the highest-priority changes with an agile approach in each sprint, and demonstrates its implementation during a sprint review with all stakeholders.

Sandbox—A cyber security mechanism for separating running programs, usually in an effort to mitigate system failures and/or software vulnerabilities from spreading. Sandboxes are often used to execute untested or untrusted programs or code.

Self-service business digital platform—A multi-purpose hub that helps an organization coordinate work and support business interactions between people and technology. Such a platform helps build a single source of truth for an organization in an efficient way.

Single source of truth (SSOT)—The central enterprise data repository of an organization, which provides it with a singular and comprehensive view of the business and its customers. The SSOT, which helps organizations to communicate in a ubiquitous language using specific common data points, provides the ability to be proactive and drive growth across sales, marketing, pricing, and operations.

Sprint—In agile software development frameworks, a sprint is a repeatable, fixed timeframe during which a product of the highest possible value is created. Sprint is a core component of the agile methodology.

Technology rationalization—The process of cataloging and eliminating duplicate technology solutions used across an organization. A mature self-service digital platform helps enterprises simplify the process of standardizing useful technologies and eliminating redundant ones across processes and operations.

ABOUT THE AUTHORS

Raj Vattikuti

Raj Vattikuti is a serial entrepreneur and philanthropist who has been dedicated to solving business challenges through innovative solutions for over three decades. Raj has an innate ability to understand the changing landscape that businesses face and adeptly cuts through the complexity by providing groundbreaking solutions that simplify business models using data and technology. With a focus on digital business, Raj has used his customer-focused mindset to transform clients' businesses.

In 1985, Raj founded Complete Business Solutions to help companies solve difficult business challenges that other firms avoided. Later renamed Covansys and listed on NASDAQ, Raj sold the business in 2007 for $1.3 billion, it had grown from five employees to 8,000. Other successful business ventures founded by Raj include Synova Inc., Vattikuti Technologies, Vattikuti Ventures, Davinta Technologies, and most recently Altimetrik in 2012.

Raj has worked with large enterprises, midsize companies, and startups throughout his career, and he has a deep understanding of the complexities and challenges they face. This was the catalyst for starting Altimetrik whose focus is on simplifying business, eliminating silos, creating a single source of truth (SSOT), and sparking innovation to realize unlimited opportunities. Utilizing practitioners, who take a business view, the company helps clients develop solutions that achieve tangible results and growth with speed. Altimetrik has grown into a pure play digital business and digital technology transformation company, partnering with dozens of clients across the globe with over 5,000 practitioners spanning 18 offices and development centers worldwide.

Raj was recognized as a 2020–2021 Entrepreneurship and Innovation Hall of Fame Inductee at Wayne State University, acknowledged as an EY Entrepreneur Of The Year® 2020 National Award winner and the Michigan and Northwest Ohio regional award winner. He is the recipient of the TiE Detroit 2017 Lifetime Achievement Award, 2007 Woodrow Wilson Award for Corporate Citizenship, 2002 Ellis Island Medal of Honor, and Dykema Gossett 2001 Lifetime Achievement Award and holds an Honorary Doctorate in Business Administration from Bryant College.

Raj believes in giving back to the communities he lives and works in. That is why he started the Vattikuti Foundation with his wife, Padma, to support cancer research and treatment programs at Henry Ford Hospitals (Vattikuti Urology Institute) and Beaumont Hospitals (Vattikuti Digital Breast Imaging Center) in Michigan. The Vattikuti Urology Institute offers the most advanced treatments for prostate cancer, kidney disease, bladder cancer, and other urologic diseases surpassing 10,000 robotic procedures used by urologic surgeons around the world. He also founded the Poverty Alleviation and Development initiative focused on health, education, and employment in rural India.

Ram Charan

In his work with companies including Toyota, Bank of America, Key Bank, ICICI Bank, Aditya Birla Group, Novartis, Max Group, Yildiz Holdings, UST Global, Fast Retailing (Uniqlo), Humana, Matrix, Longfor and two of the four largest digital companies in China, he is known for cutting through the complexity of running a business in today's fast changing environment to uncover the core business problem.

His real-world solutions, shared with millions through his books and articles in top business publications, have been praised for being practical, relevant, and highly actionable—the kind of advice you can use Monday morning. Jack Welch, former Chairman of GE said, "He has the rare ability to distill meaningful from meaningless and transfer it to others in a quiet, effective way."

Professor Charan has coached more than a dozen leaders who went on to become CEOs. He reaches many more up-and-coming business leaders through in-house executive education programs. His energetic, interactive teaching style has won him several awards, including the Bell Ringer award at GE's famous Crotonville Institute and best teacher award at Northwestern.

He was among Business Week's top ten resources for in-house executive development programs. Ram has authored or coauthored more than 30 books that have sold over 4 million copies in more than a dozen languages. Four of his books were Wall Street Journal bestsellers, including Execution (coauthored with former Honeywell CEO Larry Bossidy), which spent more than 150 weeks on the New York Times bestseller list. He also has written for publications including over 12 articles for Harvard Business Review, 12 articles for Fortune, and numerous articles for BusinessWeek, Time, Chief Executive, and USA TODAY.

Ram was elected a Distinguished Fellow of the National Academy of Human Resources and was named one of the most influential people in corporate governance and the board room by Directorship magazine. He has served on the Blue Ribbon Commission on Corporate Governance and serves or has served on a dozen boards in the US, Brazil, China, India, Canada, and Dubai.

ONE LAST THOUGHT

As organizations move into post-pandemic times, it is important to keep in mind that some of the business trends brought on by the worldwide health crisis are here to stay. The new developments go beyond the rise of virtual meetings and growth of ecommerce. The pandemic has transformed businesses, accelerating changes already underway or bringing attention to shifts that were long overdue.

Among the key business trends that might have staying power is that customer loyalty is no longer reliable. The disruption of business lockdowns forced many customers to try out new brands, even if they are not unhappy with the old ones. Any company that hopes to retain clients' need to emphasize building a simple and intuitive customer experience. This includes the use of customized content, video chat, and AI-supported text chat.

Another trend is that many organizations are now digital by default, in terms of working remotely, using digital tools to communicate, and selling products and services digitally. The term "digital transformation" is now becoming a reality—not just a buzzword. Businesses are realizing that the way they manage data, structure processes, and set up automation can be made more efficient through digital business platforms.

Digital business solutions providers can work collaboratively with companies to create resources that can serve as a single source of truth (SSOT), a central data repository that provides a singular and comprehensive view of the business and its customers. The SSOT gives businesses the ability to better track successes—and missteps—across sales, marketing, and operations. This

Scan the QR code to view case-study reference material.

allows them to be proactive in addressing problems and amplifying successes.

There is no doubt that the way businesses operate has been permanently altered, and it is likely that these changes will continue to play out in the coming years. The challenge for organizations is to embrace these changes, and leverage them to make themselves better and more agile.

Leadership Lit is an exclusive publishing imprint for CEO members of CEO Connection.

ABOUT CEO CONNECTION

CEO Connection is the only membership organization in the world reserved exclusively for CEOs of Mid-Market companies with between $100 million and $3 billion in revenue. Designed to provide you with customized and personalized access to people, information, resources, and opportunities that will enhance your career, save you time, and make you money, CEOC connects you with the people you should meet, the resources you need, and solutions to the unique challenges you face! With more than 17,000 mid-market CEOs in our community, CEOC functions as a proactive peer network where the connections are made for you.